DOWNING STREET SPECIES

By
William Tell

Published in 2012 by FeedARead.com Publishing – Arts Council funded

A CIP catalogue record for this title is available from the British Library.

CONTENTS

INTRODUCTION

The book describes a journey into the habitats of species MP with unique insight into the UK political world. The author met three Prime Ministers and two Chancellors of The Exchequer but was not impressed. In Liverpool the BBC asked him to do a film interview on what he would do if he was Prime Minister. He could have become a Labour Party MP but declined that invitation. His experiences started with a request to present to New Labour HQ on how to mobilise the 360,000 party members to win the General Election. Those experiences as unpaid strategy adviser and many more provide a unique insight into the powerbroker species. When he asked a Minister for more public monies for children's and adult hospices the Government Health Minister replied that hospices *did very well at fundraising* and therefore *didn't need support.*

The author was described by Cherie Blair/Booth as her *email friend* after the Blair's departed Downing Street. Cherie Blair who in their brief meetings laughed at his jokes was a conduit by email into No 10, but Prime Minister Blair was not for turning on Iraq, MP standards, economic management and other issues. The political legacy is still burdening people in the UK and abroad. The author presents to all people and emerging democracies a proposed blueprint for achieving political and democratic excellence.

We are all species, but it seems that many of the 650 or so Westminster MPs have evolved a unique DNA. This seeks to secure their lifestyle protection and survival. A species is sometimes defined as a group of organisms that can interbreed. Some species like the chameleon can, it seem change colour for social as well as for survival reasons in their habitats.

UK Coalition government confirms this pattern of evolution. The political class collectively has created a system that failed the people in recent political history. The people are now urged to take the lead and evolve such a system as described in the blueprint, which puts people first and truly reflects the just will and democratic rights of the people.

A 16 year journal is presented, with key years as insider, from the rise and fall of the New Labour project to the Coalition Government. Untold political insights experienced on a journey from the docklands of Liverpool onto Parliament and the Downing Street power base. Unique political foresight presented to the political leaders was sadly ignored with damaging consequences to follow. Measures to prevent the MP expenses scandal of 2009 were ignored by the political elite across a decade or more of contact. Tony Blair did not engage with Saddam Hussain to avert war as proposed but strangely went on to engage and embrace with another doomed dictator in Libya some years later.

Future Prime Minister Cameron and ministers also rejected democratic excellence proposals on MP standards. They could also have engaged in a proposed Conservative party led *big society* initiative but declined to practice what they later preached when in power. The author met future Chancellor George Osborne at a public meeting in 2010 who announced that his biggest achievement as an MP was to obtain a *cochlear ear implant for* a young constituent. Future Prime Minister Gordon Brown was warned by the author about the failure of IT/Computer systems strategy in the health service.

Then costing the taxpayer up to £1 billion. In 2009 the reported taxpayer loss in public IT systems escalated to a staggering £26 billion of waste and scrapped systems.

In June 2007 the author again warned Downing Street about the £billions of taxpayer monies wasted but the damaging economic legacy spiralled upwards. The species, the world stage players, went on to pursue their path immersed in the jungle of politics. Citizens wait in vain for greatness in leadership and government to emerge.

There are however many principled, dedicated and hard working MPs in the Westminster enclave. However Westminster has yet to deliver world class democratic leadership, to fully engage with the people and produce reform to meet the just needs of the electorate. Democracy and political service standards can be transformed and revitalised by practical and achievable initiatives. This will only be achieved if the support and will for positive change is mobilised by the people.

Extracts From Dialogue with 10 Downing Street and MPs:

19th February 2003

Pre-Iraq invasion proposal.

........My proposal is that he (The Prime Minister) takes the initiative/turns the situation around by flying out to Iraq and speaking directly with the dictator in search of a solution acceptable to Britain and America. If there is a small chance that this provides a solution then he should grasp the opportunity. If Saddam fails to respond then nobody can say that Tony did not, at some risk make an attempt at the 11th hour.

(Note: Some years later it was reported that Sir Richard Branson had a plane on standby to fly Branson and Nelson Mandela to Iraq to broker a peaceful solution to avoid bloodshed – with full approval from UN Secretary Kofi Annan. However the US/UK bombing started before they could fly out. ....In later years Blair flew out to Libya and embraced a *sanatised* dictator Ghadaffi who also had weapons of *mass destruction, supported terrorists etc*........).

8th June 2003

..........Perhaps when you move from Downing St you may consider a Blair/Booth Foundation to carry on the good work you are doing on a national/international level.

14th February 2004

New Labour Failures to address:

..........Parliamentary accountability has been whittled away by many different methods. This needs to be recovered and confidence rebuilt.

.........Although as a Christian I support a multi-ethnic society the economic migrant issue and shambles that it is will be a major factor in bringing down this Government. ....

18th February 2004

..........With respect I believe that the PM may leave office considered as a good PM but will if things don't change will miss that wonderful opportunity he had to be considered as a great PM.

12th June 2005

.............Perhaps the Prime Minister should review Standards in the House and work towards a system whereby all MPs are paid a new rate and consultancies and acquired directorships/nepotism etc in office are forbidden ?) please see attached. (The Democracy Trust MP Code Of Conduct)

5th March 2006

.... but am disappointed in the legacy the Blair years will be leaving behind. My fear for their future is that democracy has been eroding away with our hard one freedoms haemorrhaging under the new labour project. ....

...............More control on our freedoms, a green light for the use of torture by third parties, law making by the unelected, the weakening of the judiciary, rewards for the party contributors of wealth and a blind eye to declining standards in public life - now much worse than under Tory rule.

.............Near to your heart perhaps - insufficient public monies into Hospices and the care of the dying yet vast sums found to fund useless 'initiatives', computer systems, ID cards etc, etc.

1st May 2006

...................A few years ago I sent you the document below, (Note: The Democracy Trust MP Code Of Conduct) which only 26 (mostly Labour MPs endorsed in 2001). It still holds true now. I intend to resend to all MPs. Why genuine/credible/ethical politicians (including the PM who was sent a copy) could not endorse it I will never know

27st October 2006

...................How is your new book/diaries progressing.....?

9th June 2007

.........On a macro level this world is not a safer place, nor a more democratic place with Blairism but on the contrary the Blair Legacy leaves us all with more fears, more concerns and less freedom than in May 1997. Your heart must concur with me even though your logic may rush to defend the outcomes of the last decade. A successful economy founded on a Tory economic base saw many more billions spent, but badly invested on public services. A feel good factor by the many not a counter-balance to the mismanagement by Government of' initiatives, which have ended in waste and doubtful outcomes, nationally and globally.

26th June 2007

....................I have, however enjoyed my visits to Downing Street etc and experiencing the historic Blair journey since 1995. Travelling through the valleys over the over high mountains and through storm cloud weather and rainbows as it were. I do hope the new chapters in your life/Blair Foundation etc are written for the good of many and not for the few.

By a strange coincidence that evening, on the day my email headed *The Real Cherie* was sent to Cherie it was announced that a programme featuring the Prime Minister's wife was to be shown the following Wednesday night. Its title was *The Real Cherie*. (Also by another strange co-incidence my mention of rainbow in my last email was to be somewhat prophetic as a rainbow appeared over Tony Blair's constituency during the Blair's farewell visit, much to the amusement of the assembled world media).

Extracts from email sent to then Shadow Home Secretary following meeting etc:

27th March 2009

The electorate/the country is looking for politicians to live in the real world and conduct their lives subject to selfless not selfish standards. Will Cameron, Chris Grayling and colleagues have the drive and courage to take actions to reform political standards to meet the needs of all the people ? ....Self interest is a hollow, short term high. Politics should be about making a positive difference in people's lives that are served. Too many politicians from all parties put self - interest first. David Cameron may engage with a hung Parliament next election, he may make a good Prime Minister. If he immediately reforms the greed and sleaze simmering on for a decade or more in Parliament he will go on to be a great Prime Minister...

Extracts from letter and democratic opinion survey sent to all MPs 1st August 2011:

We are contacting all MPs to seek participation/feedback and support on proposals to further develop the UK democratic and political system as a world-class benchmark/model. The objective, hopefully with your support is to promote democratic renewal with new initiatives based on a defined framework and developed 'Investor In Democracy' standards. The aim is to facilitate greater participation by the electorate in democracy and to promote enhanced political standards, service and outcomes. This initiative would be supported by a proposed covenant* (enclosed) for MPs, Councillors etc.

Although the current Westminster MP code is currently under review we believe that a separate citizen focused code or covenant will add value to this process and should be considered. *(As code presented to all 659 MPs in 2001 by the Democracy Trust).

Code of conduct – re-presented to 650 MPs in 2011 for endorsement 1st August 2011: **(As of 1st January 2012 only 2 MPs had signed up to the code................)**

Proposed Standard/Code Of Conduct: Members Of Parliament

As a holder or prospective holder of public office I promise to support, promote and uphold at all times the following standards:

1. To act solely in the public interest as specified within the seven principles of public life* in both spirit and compliance: Selflessness, Integrity, Objectivity, Accountability, Openness, Honesty and Leadership. *(The Nolan/Neill Committee recommendations - House Of Commons on standards In Public Life.

2. To comply with in terms of accuracy, compliance, timeliness and without mis-interpretation all current standards and codes of conduct including register of interests and statutory requirements of the appropriate public office.

3. To preserve existing democratic processes and promote development of enhanced democratic processes in all aspects of public life and politics in particular.

4. To support the rights and democratic will of the people I serve, unswayed by inappropriate commercial, career or political pressures.

5. To protect and uphold the principles of rule of law, respect for all people, valuing and protecting human rights, liberty, freedom of expression and democracy.

6. To respect and uphold the principles of equal opportunity in all matters of public office and for all the people served by me.

7. To respect and uphold appropriate protection of the countryside and environment in the area I serve and the world in general.

8. Not to seek or accept personal financial benefit or gifts in kind other than those, which are intended to be

passed over in their entirety to the benefit of the broader community with no gain to myself, family, or friends.

9. In respect of above I will accept no new remunerated directorships or consultancy roles after taking up public office except roles directly benefiting the community and not adversely affecting my input to, or performance in public service.

10. To provide regular and open access to the people I serve to make full use of my services and to hold me to account. This could be in the form of regular and confidential surgeries or public forums to meet the needs of the people served.

11. To uphold the principles of freedom of information and openness at all times and encourage others to scrutinise inappropriate activities of public concern.

12. Be committed to working within a ethical and moral framework in public office to promote and deliver benefits to people both locally and in the wider world community

ACKNOWLEDGEMENTS

With gratitude and love to my mother, father and other such selfless people in the community of life who provided the basis of what politics should be about. That is to selflessly work towards making a positive difference in the lives of others.

With thanks and much love and appreciation to my wife, daughters, son, family and friends, who are much loved and supported me in so many ways over the years. My love will last as long as the stars shine bright in the dark sky above.

Many thanks also to the medical staff and teams who saved my life so many times over the years and provided so many more chapters in my life since the morning of the Friday 13th November 1992 when my heart stopped. Reborn with a spirit strengthened for the years to follow. Thanks also for those who provided much support in producing this book.

THE AUTHOR

William has always believed that life is about working towards making a positive difference in the lives of others. That belief has been with him since an early age. Recognising that we all have strengths, weaknesses and human frailties he believes that adding value to other people's lives is a key goal worth working for. William enjoyed a loving, caring working class family childhood close to the docklands in Liverpool, UK and lived in a small council house. This was at times a home also to budgerigars, a large owl, hens, various reptiles and pets. A nocturnal home also to armies of cockroaches, which invaded the ground floor rooms when the lights were turned off at night. William is an identical twin, one of the seven children in the family.

His mother toiled in local factories or cleaned pub toilets and bars to support the family. His dad hurt his spine whilst working as a dock labourer and suffered both the disability and the financial consequences. However there was always food to eat, second hand clothing mostly to wear and cramped caravan holidays by the seaside when it was affordable. Sadly his elder brother George drowned in a local canal just before William and his twin brother were born. His mother lost one son and gave birth to the unexpected twins.

By fate, luck or good fortune William went on, albeit not too heroically, in four different situations to save four people from drowning during his lifetime. That included saving a young boy in the same canal where his older brother died some 13 years before. That is one of many episodes of unusual lifetime experiences (Book – ***Strong Spirit, Weak Heart***) including identical twin tales, psychic happenings and more. Many such events witnessed/validated by independent and credible people. Some later to manifest during his participation in politics. He was to survive seven or more life threatening medical conditions and around thirty surgical operations or procedures. He is a psychic who has had many unexplained insights since his near death experience. Insights and predictions into future events, the lives of others as witnessed by many credible people like a senior figure in a Government Ministry, Solicitors, Doctors, Nurses, College Tutor and many others. He had specific insight into the southern England Milly Dowler murder tragedy before the case details were made public and was asked to participate in a psychic research short film for the Channel 4 TV Richard and Judy Show.

From poor roots he progressed from apprentice engineer to management consultancy and adviser to politicians, the public, private and not for profit sectors. His career role took him to Downing Street, UK/European Parliament, China and across the UK advising individuals, business start-ups, PLCs, the NHS, national and local companies, charities and a major political party. He co-founded The Democracy Trust in 2000. William is married with five children and four grandchildren.

The Author had many book titles in mind before he chose **Downing Street Species** as this title. That name was chosen many months before the first rodent in the form of a rat was filmed running across the doorstep of No 10 Downing Street on January 17th 2011. This rodent was followed shortly afterwards by mice infestation in 10 Downing Street in the months to follow as witnessed by Prime Minister Cameron.

In this book the species politician, whether in Downing Street or Parliament definitely have no inferred linkage to the rats or other rodents that share the habitat of Downing Street with the powerbrokers.

All net revenue after costs for this book will be invested in not for profit community support initiatives including common good projects, democratic development initiatives and proactive support to individuals, hospices, charities, small businesses/social enterprises etc.

1

THE ROAD TO DOWNING STREET

During my 16 year journey into habitats political it became clear that although many of the UK people's representatives had vision and hopes that they were subsumed by the jungle of politics and tribal conflict. Survival and dominance for many in their species meant embracing new shades of colour and sometimes suppression of natural instincts. For example the party whip system used blatantly to suppress true democratic representation of the people.

A force clearly demonstrated in October 2011 when party whip pressures on MPs meant that the commons vote on having a citizen referendum on EU membership was lost. This was blatantly against the democratic will of the people and at odds with many opinion polls showing majority public support for a referendum. However the 111 cross party MPs who truly represented the people at that vote showed immense integrity and democratic accountability.

In the time I have participated in politics I became to believe as many others now do that true representative democracy in Westminster is an aspiration rather than a reality. I, like others question whether we really do have a world class democracy in this country. Do politicians collectively reflect the just will of the electorate? Have politicians gained the trust of the people and as a group demonstrated selfless public service as defined in Parliaments *Seven Principles of Public Life*?

To those questions the electorate would undoubtedly reply with a resounding no. Is there a way forward to upgrade our political and democratic systems and can it be achieved?

Yes it can is the answer and it is not a rocket science approach. There are practical and achievable solutions available to meet the expectations of the people. However species political with others in the Westminster enclave must embrace change and support positive development for the common good. Parliament should and can regain respect as the *mother of all Parliaments.* It can become a world class model of democratic standards and excellence for the rest of the world and developing/emerging democracies.

On visits to 10 and 11 Downing Street, meeting MPs and Ministers and onto Brussels it became clear that too many politicians failed to represent the democratic will and just expectations of the people. Flawed political leadership with failures by MPs to manage public monies resulted in poor government. Opposition parties often failing to hold government to account. Recent political history showed that some governments could not organise a drinks party in a brewery. Cherie Blair got that analysis and particular message from me on 1st May 2006.

Whether she passed that frank opinion about the Labour Government onto Prime Minister Tony Blair I will never know. The MP species across the political spectrum were quick to point the finger of blame for the full economic disaster facing the UK in 2010 and beyond. Yet as representatives of the people since 1997 all 659 MPs collectively had an ongoing duty of care. A duty to hold to account, to question, highlight and seek to address mismanagement of the economy and public monies on behalf of their constituents.

Massive job losses and cuts in services and community support now presented as the result of the past Labour Government policies. Coalition scrutiny of the country's balance sheets and liabilities appearing in 2010 as revelations.

The economic *legacy* of Labour presented by the coalition as newly discovered although having 13 years of opportunity to hold the Government to account. 13 years to scrutinise the books, to challenge, to utilise value for money reviews, audit commission resources and public opinion.

It is akin to the Lib Dem/Conservative coalition saying that they have just discovered that Father Christmas doesn't exist and they just didn't know until then. All MPs as the Board of UK Plc must hold full responsibility for the massive challenges facing the electorate and their children. The lesson is clearly that irresponsible spending and waste of public monies is never again allowed to spiral out of control. The Downing Street species over the last decade or so, including the Cabinets, the Prime Ministers, the Chancellors and those MPs enjoying the hospitality/benefits of Downing Street and Westminster clearly have lessons to learn. Blame to share in that legacy facing the nation. It was not impossible to deliver what they were elected to do with an ethical and business-like approach, securing value for taxpayers money for the common good.

I last enjoyed my last Downing Street hospitality in 2007 but it was just glasses of water. Sober that time on my return visit to No 10 for one of the final farewell parties of the Blair/Booth decade of power I walked out of that famous doorway into the real world. I had on that visit turned down the alcohol and canapés as I become fuelled with frustration at the surreal celebration still underway within the great rooms of political history. BBC presenter Fiona Bruce had ignored a major issue raised when she had interviewed me at No 10 an hour or so before. That relates to another story, which follows of positive and negative forces, faith, hope, charity and despair. I once told ex-

email friend Cherie Blair that I would have walked over burning hot coals to support Tony Blair's New Labour vision of politics for the people. However, the savage cuts inflicted and planned by the 2010/11 UK Coalition Government across public services with nation-wide job losses demonstrates the impact of politician led unsound economic strategy. Now as fallen disciple of Blair the leader, *ex-email friend* of Cherie/Vice President.... I walked away from a decade or more of Labour party political promises discarded. Pledges and contracts with the people unmet.

Promises like the *purer than pure* political pledge, a *stakeholder society for all*, economic *prudence*, a party delivering for *the many, not the few*. All just words now confined to a list of pledges unfulfilled. A democratic system tainted also by spin as black clouds, false dawns, missed opportunities and visions unravelled. Democracy benefiting the few at the top, not the many in all stratas of society. Politics failing a once proud people's party seeking social justice. A political force later outvoted, impotent, to linger in opposition as the coalition government weaves its web in 2010 and beyond. Inter-breeding, colours merging in the political species. Survive they must.

Walking out of Downing Street with me on my last visit were three unsung community angels who against the odds had enriched the lives of many others in need. The Big Society announced by David Cameron already alive and well in that trio before David's time had come. Whilst some politicians elected to serve had been shown to enrich the lives of the few - e.g. their own bank accounts the angels had made a positive difference to many in need. I had obtained Downing Street invitations for the angels after good friend and community activist Rob Lloyd and I made a £770 donation to the hospice charity of which Cherie Blair was Vice President. We politely walked out the doorway of 10 Downing Street on May 2nd 2007 with a farewell to Cherie Blair and so it seemed her fan club, charity guests and MPs. I was leaving to take more steps on the journey of political insight and incredulity that started a decade or so before. A year or so later back in Liverpool, the home-town for Cherie Blair I again met Cherie. She was to write, *to Bill* my *email friend* in her book *Speaking For Myself* and handed me that copy. I was now officially an ex email friend of Cherie Booth. The blunt words I suggested she should write in her book were dismantled by her broad smile. My suggestion that she write *To Bill my pain in the ass email friend* rejected as she said I was polite most of the time.

On returning home that night I started reading her 400 page book beginning with her roots in Liverpool, her success in the legal profession and onto the world stage. However, I admit I gave up reading her book less than halfway through. Sorry Cherie I thought, I plead guilty to boredom - your honour. I filed the book on the shelf and there it stayed. During my email contacts with her over a five year period or so Cherie told me that some of my political proposals had been passed to Tony. However Tony was not a man for turning. Perhaps one scouser in the form of Cherie was enough for him to contend with in respect of advice to change the world.

Amongst my many opinions, supportive as well as critical that I presented to Cherie I suggested that her husband, if continuing on the same path may be considered *as a good Prime Minister, but never a great Prime Minister*. Following my suggestion that her husband's Government could not organise a drinks party in a brewery she reminded me how great things were after she had opened new children's centres that

27

week in Newcastle. She said the fantastic facilities would not have happened but for New Labour policies. However my frank opinions with my other views on Prime Minister Blair's term in office did not prevent that particular invitation to 10 Downing Street to enjoy a farewell party. Albeit a drinks party not held in a brewery.

Blair/Booth and Brown once unknown, ordinary faces in the crowd had been subjected to a decade or more of extraordinary scrutiny by the media, the people of this country and to some extent by myself. As one of Blair's stakeholders, Blair disciple even, since 1995 I became subsequent contributor to national and regional modernisation of the party, mentor to some knights and soldiers in the Blair crusade. I had been invited to many high level events including the European Parliament and visits to 10/11 Downing Street. This included a giggly wine filled afternoon for me with the then Chancellor Gordon Brown and others. I was later to avoid the alcohol at the event with Cherie Blair to enjoy a sober appraisal of her singing followed by my brief but frank interview with BBC TVs, Fiona Bruce.

My friends and I left the film crew, the great, the good, the MPs, the mere mortals with canapés and fine wine still partying at the historic terraced house behind us. The singing of Cherie Blair and her ex-schoolmates ringing on in our ears like a karaoke session led by posh scouse with would be tribute band nice girls. Sadly, without choreography or indeed the harmony. Most unlikely to make Pop Idol, Britain's Got Talent and definitely lacking the X Factor. The jolly old school song from Cherie Blair's school days perhaps entertaining to some present. They who responded with smiles to the BBC camera crew. Leaving No 10 with me were three tireless heroes of their communities, all who had faced challenges and adversity with courage and selfless endeavours. Two men and one woman, steadfast still without politics positively impacting on their life mission to make a difference in the lives of others. Dedicated and delivering with distinction practical, positive support on a daily basis for people in need.

Actions more effective than the fine words and the opportunities wasted by some of the hierarchy of New Labour over the previous decade. Many politicians whom had put self first and public service last. There was sadness and deep frustration inside of me and others in that great Downing Street room. Sadness because of decisions implemented but now off the agenda it seemed at the No 10 reception. My brief interview with words spoken on and off-camera with BBCs' Fiona Bruce that evening never to be broadcast. No mention of my concerns in the TV programme The Real Cherie, screened shortly afterwards about her Downing Street life, her historic role, which gave access to the film crew. I was a Blair disciple, a Blair/Booth pen-pal no more.

The policeman on the door, more pleasant than any night club doorman had joked with us and bade a sincere farewell as we returned to the world beyond the gates of the historic street. I had also reached the end of a road with Mrs Blair I thought but was yet to meet her again in 2009 and 2010. Was it Ms Booth or Mrs Blair I thought and who was the Real Cherie. Perhaps her long awaited autobiography would fully describe the Cherie of many roles.

Walking away from the world of political strife, ambition, power and wealth my friends and I stepped back into the real world. A world still yearning for great leaders to bring light into dark places, providing hope for the many. Further chapters were yet to unfold as the gate closed firmly to secure the famous street. I walked away with a clear vision intact, but still unmet on what Tony Blair's New Labour *third way* could and should have been. I found Blairism in the final decade of the last millennium and willingly became a Blair disciple. It began as a journey of hope and optimism following despair at tired right wing politics. Hopes dashed over those years with my eventual rejection of the discredited new politics. So many promises unfulfilled by New Labour who perhaps had the vision but not the ability to deliver what was preached. I had always believed that politicians should have selfless aims and responsibilities to deliver.

Aims indeed as those Tony Blair and John Prescott had once preached about New Labour being the much quoted brother's keeper for the common good. I believed that politics was all about addressing the need in the world, managing resources and making a positive difference in people's lives. We all have a life mission and politicians have their part to play for the greater good. I believed passionately that we were all created equal and that one person's actions could as a pebble thrown into the world pond create a ripple affect to reach out for the greater good. Politicians are entrusted with the power to throw boulders as well as small pebbles of positive or negative change into the world pond to great effect.

Yet many politicians stayed on the edges unwilling to create any movement or make waves whilst taking the people's monies and benefits. Politicians and non-politicians like Nelson Mandela, Martin Luther King, Mother Theresa, Winston Churchill and countless other individuals were once ordinary people until they moved, made waves and took a place in world history. Sadly both Blair and Gordon Brown it seems will never be considered as great Prime Ministers. The third Prime Minister I was to meet as opposition leader - David Cameron whom I met a few years before he took up office was still on the launch pad of his journey of political history making.

Reforming our political system is indeed not rocket science and in-touch politicians who reflect the reasonable will of the people and show high quality leadership and innovation can take their place in historic political nostalgia or just as quickly be erased from the electorate's memory. The jury is not yet summoned for Cameron/Clegg coalition but I do believe the potential is there for David Cameron if he breaks the mould of the old politics and embraces a new democratic and political blueprint. For it to succeed it must be designed for the many, not the few. It must meet the just needs of the people and be truly accountable to the people.

I was sadly to discover on my political journey that the British political ruling class consisted of too many self-serving, patronising, out of touch so called honourable members, allegedly servants of the people. Too many politicians appeared to put self first before the greater good of society. I walked away from a possible career as MP because of those reasons and my concerns on democratic erosion. The Daily Telegraph confirmed my opinion on MP so called standards and became the voice of the people exposing the greed of many politicians. Many MPs in 2009/10 were to face the outrage of the electorate by both public opinion and ballot box.

I often wondered how some career MPs would manage in the real world as job-seekers? Bending the rules, accounting errors by some of the political class was evident to me and others many years back before that particular scandal dominated the media, but that is another story. In 2001 some 633 MPs rejected my think tank's (Democracy Trust) proposed code of conduct for

MPs, which sought to address the MP expense time-bomb scenario. This was designed to encourage MPs to embrace enhanced higher standards of selfless service in public life. It consisted of an electorate focused pledge benchmarked by high standards.

It meant MPs not taking up other jobs, directorships etc, nor acquiring financial gain from office, or employing family members. It included regular review/evaluation by their Constituents, freedom of information compliance and working in a moral and ethical framework etc. However 26 MPs did endorse that code. Twelve of those MPs were however to face scrutiny by the Daily Telegraph for their expense/allowance claims some eight years or so later. One MP allegedly claimed back £5 for a church service collection and another MP allegedly attempted to claim £1049 for a TV as he was allegedly too busy to shop around.

My hopes, as for millions of other UK citizens on that day in May 1997 when New Labour became a Government were dashed as the years passed and politics failed the people. The dream team Blair, Brown and Prescott delivered a New Labour strategy, which would include the Iraq and Afghan wars, the credit crunch economy, a legacy of unbelievable debt for UK citizens. The MPs/Parliament and their public servants collectively allowed greed to flourish, which resulted in the MP expenses scandal in 2009, resulting in electorate outrage. Revelations about MPs with so-called *snouts in the trough* would become world-wide news and even be used as a propaganda tool by the Iranian Ayatollahs.

In contrast when Labour was in opposition they waged principled but now it transpires hypocritical campaigning in the form of sustained snouts in the trough campaigns against Tory policy re, privatised companies such as British Gas etc for employing directors on high salaries and benefits.

During my political journey with the political stars I had brief encounters and more with the good, the bad and the ugly at many stratas in the political bedrock. Warm hearted people like Sir Christopher Meyer, ex- Ambassador to the USA and ex MP Neil with his wife Christine Hamilton were to offer much welcome encouragement to me. Neil wrote to me to say that truth was stranger than fiction, which based on the experiences I will later relate, was quite prophetic. Jeremy Paxman from BBC 2 Newsnight was to send me his book with the words *I hear you have been plotting in my office*? Two high profile political figures referred to me as their *guru* as they took my advice whilst I kept my hidden fears and self-doubts from them during our meetings. Perhaps many of us feel the fear but play our part in life's interaction and careers. Another William once wrote life is a stage, and he was spot on.

I found it encouraging however that for many who failed their eleven plus exam like me (and Deputy Prime Minister John Prescott with all his strengths and weaknesses) and against many life challenges that ordinary people can move on to develop roles in politics, in the commercial world and more and thus have opportunity to try to make a positive impact in life. Making the most of the opportunities that present is the key and being positive and proactive. By luck or fate I went on in my lifetime to develop various opportunities including advising business, captains of industry, the NHS, the not for profit sector, some in the political establishment and even a formidable reformed ex-drug dealer now working for the community. He was really scary but sometimes gave me a big hug when we met.

As long as he didn't try to kiss me that was ok I decided. My lifetime opportunities took me to both doors of Downing Street, to the European Parliament and on to China, where I reluctantly danced with male Chinese politicians. I also sang unchained melody to students at a Chinese university, with a UK trade mission in the audience. The audience included a UK coffin manufacturer looking for opportunities, various north- west political insiders and now sadly deceased Tony Wilson, TV broadcaster and music entrepreneur.

Cherie Blair was later to follow my lead some years later to sing a Beatles song to some students in her China visit as filmed by the world media. She made international news. I did not make the news of course. Liverpool culture/scouse talent had travelled east at last I thought. One of us did sing out of tune however and I got there first to set the scene for Merseyside X Factor. I believe that life provides choice and opportunity for us all in this world. I believe in destiny blended with choice and that we all have a life mission to fulfil. Politicians more so than any of us have a unique life mission role because of the power and influence entrusted in them.

Some eight years after my MP code was proposed and following the MP expenses scandal in 2009 Prime Minister Brown and Opposition Leader David Cameron said they were considering a code of conduct for MPs. Too little too late perhaps as many of the electorate now hold politicians in contempt for abusing the trust placed with them. The question is whether the party leaders will deliver an MP code of conduct, which is independently monitored, which satisfies the people of this country in terms of appropriate substance and is backed up with remedial measures and penalties for non-compliance.

Along my journey of discovery of that human nature peculiar to the elected elite I had presented political initiatives via local, regional, national and European platforms. My citizen suggestion via Cherie Blair to No 10 (she said: she would pass it on) to seek to prevent the Iraq war was discounted. I found out years later that Sir Richard Branson had formulated a similar strategy with Nelson Mandela. The initiative was approved by UN Secretary General Kofi Annan, but was sadly foiled by the US rush to war when bombing commenced. Hundreds of thousands or more people had paid the price in death, injury and other horrors for the failure to use peaceful means to remove Saddam. The carnage continues to this day with car bombings killing the innocents and creating life long pain and suffering for those family members suffering losses of loved ones.

Maybe I was too idealistic in my vision for optimum Government strategy for the common good. I was born in Liverpool, my birth sign, as a so-called perfectionist Virgo alongside my identical twin. At our birth however, a twenty-minute delay in my coming meant I was certainly the younger and I would argue the better looking twin. Observing each others strengths and weaknesses in the following decades was the price paid for being twins and questions about twin telepathy still get asked of us. We both went on to have careers providing support and advice to individuals and large organisations in most sectors of the profit and not for profit sector.

Along the way I fitted in being a serial survivor against the odds. Close encounters with life threatening challenges many times. I, whilst seeking to achieve my life mission became almost by accident a political insider for a short but significant period in recent political history. I came from a spirit rich, but pocket poor working class family of seven children who used cobbled streets by the docks and the paths and shore of the River Mersey as a playground.

Our dad was a docker who hurt his spine working on those docks and suffered illness and no wages for many years. He eventually died at a young 67 from asbestosis originating from his sea-going and dockside working life. Mam worked as a lowly paid cleaner in a local pub, but to her and dad happiness was free, having no price ticket. Cherie Blair, a fellow scouser lived a twenty minute walk away and must also have tread our local paths alongside the concrete pill box fortifications still standing on the beaches and dockland after the war years. Her book describes her poor background but to our family she lived in much more of a posh area. Much later in life we were to exchange smiles, a photograph, handshakes and emails lasting from before the Iraq war to the Blair's leaving of Downing Street some years later and up to 2010.

Sadly for me in the last weeks of the Blair tenancy in Downing Street my email friend Cherie did not respond to my personal appeals for her high profile help and support to publicly support me and campaigners to halt the closure of one of two faith based Jospice charity hospice services that Cherie was Vice-President of in her hometown - near Liverpool. Many like me were disappointed and saddened that Cherie allegedly never did visit the threatened Ormskirk hospice site of her charity to listen to the campaign business-people with proposals, the local staff, volunteers and patients' families had to say.

(The hospice charity was founded by a charismatic catholic priest, whose hospice motto was - *whilst I breathe I hope*). I breathed, I hoped but some did not share the same hope. To be fair she may have made great efforts behind the scenes to find solutions to try to prevent the hospice closure. However if that was the case the Ormskirk staff, patients, their families and campaigners were unaware of that fact. In response to our campaign TV impressionist Jon Culshaw offered support and went on the *Who Wants to be a Millionaire* show and raised over £10,000 for the hospice. My wife and I were to meet him some years later in May 2010 and to thank him personally for his kindness. He did visit the doomed Ormskirk hospice but Cherie allegedly did not. *I'm a Celebrity Get Me Out of Here!* - Christine Hamilton spoke to me and gave me a letter of support for the media campaign.

Despite our best efforts Cherie's charity trustees decided to close the hospice site and relocate the surviving patients. Patients effectively being evicted and relocated had no legal remedy available to prevent the closure of that place of love and care. That is a story that could (I believe) have had a more positive outcome for a long established centre of excellence for hospice care in Lancashire if the collective will had been mobilised. A gifted lady philosopher and psychic at the London College of psychic studies once told me that life is not about success or failure, it is about experience.

That failed campaign, the experience over the months certainly involved politics, personalities, passion and choices made by individuals, which revealed the goodness of many, the heartache and the clash of the positive and negative forces. Back to international, national politics and economic management. Prime Minister Blair left a mixed legacy including of course his and Gordon Brown's pitiful support for hospices in the care of the dying. Many wasted opportunities of the power entrusted and as it transpired a questionable succession plan. On my political journey I had gained insight into what some in the party would undertake in the pursuit of power, when money was not a constraint and political strategy just had to be met.

Perhaps some politicians believed that the end result justified the means and that self-serving politics would always be tolerated by the prolonged feel good economic factor then enjoyed by the electorate. Now fading from memory as coalition economic policies take hold. A world of millions sought inspired actions by politicians to give hope to the many and to champion solutions for planet mankind. Blair was part of the solution but also part of the problem. A legacy was written for outgoing Prime Minister Blair by the few for the many. Written as an analogy, I would compare Tony Blair (and indeed Gordon Brown) as a Captain to a ship now lost in stormy waters. A promised precious cargo now submerged without reaching its final port or haven. Many souls lost on the journey and survivors hanging on, frantically searching the horizon for new berths, new lives.

A newly promoted Captain Brown took charge of a different vessel but often appeared seasick and unsure of his crew-members. A Captain Brown destined to leave ship for the mountains of Scotland after facing a submarine of blue Tory colours manned by a mixed crew. A book writing sabbatical it turned out to be. Captain Cameron and navigator Clegg now on the surface preparing to torpedo any chance of the Labour Party setting sail to discharge another shifting cargo of political baggage. I had experienced a rapid transformation from New Labour foot soldier and anointed Blairite disciple, to engaging with the party hierarchy and big business.

The journey gave insight into secretive and strange political tactics, political intrigue and the effect of power on the person. It also gave me that opportunity to relay support and not so welcome political analysis and proposals across some years into No 10 via Cherie Blair. Cherie as the twelfth most powerful woman in the world according to some survey. But was it Ms Booth or Mrs Blair conversing with me from over the shop in Downing Street? Was she a fellow scouser some would ask.

That badge of origin floated on the tide to pastures new beyond the River Mersey some years before and after the world became an oyster for the Blair's I thought. I believed she was still loyal to her roots and often returned to Liverpool for worthy causes. The accent was not evident but her heart was probably still there although the Blair's wealth had provided them with many luxurious homes away from her childhood roots. Until my late forties I was mildly interested in, but not involved in politics. I had invested most of my previous years from mid-teens onwards committed to wine, women and song during the Liverpool Mersey-beat pop scene and beyond. I had little time even to follow world famous local football teams of Liverpool or Everton, never mind engaging with the electorate or party activists. However that was all to change as a result of the circumstances contributing to the death of my mother in the care of the local NHS hospital.

I was galvanised into political participation by my despair at unsound Conservative policies, which I believed resulted in health-care inequality and negative market forces foisted upon the NHS. I also had a one to one meeting with Gordon Brown and submitted a request for MPs to investigate the wasted taxpayer £millions purchasing failed NHS computer systems and expensive management consultancy. A decade or more later the prudent Chancellor, later Prime Minister, had allowed that waste of public monies to spiral upwards to now be measured in many £billions when medicines are rationed according to post-code budgets.

Also the NHS will be crippled financially for decades by the reported £65 billion or more private finance initiative (PFI) approved by the Chancellor with massive interest charges yearly paid out of the public purse for the new hospitals and services contracted to private companies. I came from a poor working class background whose parents voted Conservative, with no active participation in party politics. However mam and dad had a great interest in social matters, displayed a fighting spirit against injustice and were generally active helping others in the community.

They wanted me to do good things in life as they had tried to do. I believed politics was the right vehicle for influencing change. I admit to being flattered if that is the right description in just a short time after joining the Labour Party to be invited to London to present a high level proposal to the party general secretary, later Life Peer, Baron Sawyer in mobilising the 360,000 membership to win a general election. I wondered what true blue mam and dad would think of me providing advice to the socialist great and the good. I was later invited to present to sixty or more would- be or serving Labour MPs, pre-1997 general election and party organisers on election organisation and best-practice and winning the general election. Later to attend numerous high profile party events and to visit the European Parliament and meet MEPs.

Many events I attended would enable me snatched dialogues with Ministers and MPs as well as the Blairs. I even had a healthy debate with a female government minister in the back seat of a car. She wasn't my type though and the common sense suggestions I made to her about assisting businesses and charities were probably forgotten as soon as I closed the car door. Perhaps I had a lucky escape though and for that I was grateful. I was to later develop the link to power via Cherie in my email hot-line through to Downing Street with some of my proposals allegedly passed to the Prime Minister. This contact included attending lunches and events etc in Liverpool etc and No 10 lasting from before the Iraq war and until Blair and Booth left Downing Street and into 2010.

My wife jokingly asked me if I fancied Cherie as I was periodically in contact over the years with Cherie who was my wife's age. Once in 10 Downing Street Cherie walked over to me saying *hello Bill* and linked arms with me, which took me and other guests by surprise. My answer to my wife was no, of course I didn't fancy her. I don't suppose Tony asked Cherie a similar question of me.

During those years of contact I was sometimes supportive and often critically constructive, but to give Cherie credit she was polite at all times. She always got back to me by email and quite often within minutes of my own email. Even at the weekend she seemed to be never too far away from her computer. Over a half of her replies to me were within an hour of my sending my email. She was probably keeping a diary then and preparing for lucrative publication and sales of her inside story from a decade in Downing Street. I tried to tease out of her whether she was actually writing the book some years ago but she didn't respond to the question.

Only once did she fail to reply to emails sent and that was in her last few days at No 10. I probably pissed her off with my comments in seeking support in my campaign to stop one of her hometown hospices from being closed down. Tony Blair probably left Downing Street with much baggage and many aspirations and dreams unmet echoing to the vacated living quarters over No 11. Rooms stripped bare of personal possessions made ready for a new tenant family.

Meanwhile a country patiently waited in vain for greatness to emerge. In No 10 a new portrait of ex-PM Blair was yet to be hung on the stairwell of premier's portraits. Ex-PM Brown was to follow. A staircase gallery of those past leaders remembered for their failures or great achievements. Privileged people afforded the historic opportunity granted to them. Leaders using democracy to make a difference, but never to please all of the people all of the time. I had engaged in politics mainly out of frustration with NHS policies and what I believed was the creeping privatisation of public services. I was later to tread the engine rooms of New Labour campaign machine, bear witness to the strange standards of some up to a senior level in the Party. But that is another story.

I was asked to provide campaigning help behind the scenes on behalf of the New Labour hierarchy for the campaign in 1997 to elect the independent candidate Martin Bell. This was a high profile campaign visited by the world's media with the independent badged candidate supported by all political parties in different ways. Candidate Martin Bell fighting against the then alleged cash for questions/ brown envelopes Conservative MP Neil Hamilton.

In Tatton, Cheshire on the night of the 1997 General Election victory and until the early hours of the next day I and many more celebrated the New Labour land-slide. As well as significant Labour Party and Liberal Democrat resources some elements of the local Conservative Party with volunteers from across the country worked with me and others to ensure Tory MP Neil Hamilton lost one of the safest Tory seats in the country. When dawn was breaking on the New Labour Government and Martin Bell's victory, my wife and I walked back to our hotel from the celebration party. With us strolling across Knutsford Heath was David

Soul, the actor from the Starsky and Hutch TV series, singer and then political activist in Martin Bell's campaign. United in victory we had stars in our eyes, champagne bottles in our arms as the new sunrise bathed our weary but contented faces and emerging hangovers.

A story to tell, a surreal experience. One of many memorable experiences to follow over the next decade or so. In May 2010 I was to return to Tatton and speak to future Chancellor George Osborne MP after his hustings event to the local electorate. I chaired a similar event there with George on the platform in 2001 when he was elected as MP. We both admitted to event nerves at that time during our public appearance. There were serious times and fun days during my New Labour experience. I was to get somewhat the worse for drink at No 11 Downing Street in the company of the then Chancellor Gordon Brown. I pinched the bottom of my friend Andy, a senior political adviser he was talking to. Both nearly jumped out of their skins and I don't think Gordon has been the same since.

He still has that haunted look of post-traumatic stress I thought. I was never invited back to visit No 11, but I still have a good photograph of us both. On one photo my eyes closed as asleep standing next to Gordon. A photo I was later to show Cherie Blair many years later at No 10. In response she smiled and pulled faces at Gordon in mock disgust. At a meeting in Liverpool, ex-Northern Ireland Minister Mo Mowlam, the most human and brave Minister of them all told me a dirty joke.

Prior to that Mo was telling me about the large number of overnight stays she experienced and often forgetting where the toilet was when she woke during nights away from home. Following her lead I related a true story about my old boss in Littlewoods Plc who came from Carrickfergus in Northern Ireland. After a drunken night out on company expenses he shared a twin bedded hotel room with his boss. During the night he woke up and not knowing where he was peed all over his boss's bed. When they awoke in the morning he suggested his boss look for the offending leak in the ceiling. His boss complained to the hotel manager who was mystified. Mo Mowlam was shaking with the giggles on hearing that story. Mo went on to tell me a really rude joke. A joke I surprisingly didn't fully understand but I laughed at it anyway just as you do in situations like that. I told her another joke, which she laughed at but maybe she was just being polite with me.

Ex Mayor of London, Ken Livingston, was not to laugh at my joke when I discussed his book sales with him at a Labour Party conference. However as the saying goes I was not as pissed as his alleged much loved newts at that time. A Health Minister was to annoy me with his crass remark when I asked for more Government money for Hospices. A Government Minister was to buy me a taxpayer subsidised pint or two in Parliament in 2005, use my help and support whilst I helped him to retain his seat in Parliament. For that I didn't even get a thank you from him nor did he follow up with what he said he would do for me. Blair's guru and ex-Minister Peter Mandleson was to say hello and give me a nice smile in the men's toilet at a political meeting at Everton Football Club in Liverpool.

We shook hands and I tried to impress him with my grasp of party policy but had no wishes to grasp him if you know what I mean. I walked away hoping he had washed his hands after going the toilet. I didn't want his personal DNA on my hands. However he seemed a sincere person with a limp and somewhat damp handshake though.

In June 1995 I listened to a speech given by much travelled caravanner and Shadow Health Secretary, Margaret Beckett MP. I had a chat with her and followed up with a letter after the discussion about my views on NHS multi-million waste. This was on ineffective departmental computer systems in the NHS when wards were being closed due to lack of resources. I sent her some research I had gathered on the subject validated by experts. I had a letter back from her talking about a possible follow up, which never happened. Two years later I spoke to Gordon Brown MP in a one to one meeting on the same subject. Again a letter back from another MP with no substantive action, no common sense strategy for the future. A decade of failed computer systems right across public services was to follow during Labour's administration.

Billions of taxpayers money wasted. Talk about couldn't organise a drinks party in a brewery. The key to successful NHS IT modernisation of course was not rocket science if properly planned and implemented. The key was to fully involve the intended users of the systems in the design and development process, to set up user groups, pilot the systems, get it right and then roll out tried and tested systems. However big project failures made the headlines year on year, with some high fee earning IT and business consultancies taking £millions from front line public services.

I was for some years a loyal disciple of New Labour, later to be approved nationally as MP material. I was as a disciple to meet many of the Labour hierarchy. I decided some six years or so after joining the party not to sell my soul to pursue a seat as an on-message MP. My high level Labour endorser told me in his words that the party had enough *toady MPs*. But to his disappointment I declined to follow up a role managed by on-message political control and spin in the pursuit of a political career in Parliament. For a time I was to be a small cog in Tony Blair's promised *purer than pure* fresh new world of New Labour political standards and values declared on that day of victory outside the door of 10 Downing Street in May 1997.

A day of victory as immortalised by the eager crowd of party workers waving flags in Downing Street. Many like my party official colleague in the Tatton election had received a directive to get down to Downing Street that day. From the campaign corners of the country Labour staff had to drop everything and travel to London the next day to eagerly perform their spontaneous role as rent a crowd, joyous voters, allegedly for the world's media. A select crowd to welcome the new dawn, the new statesman with his family announcing ethical politics, or some fairy tale like that on the steps of their new Downing Street home.

A new Government was born, *the third way* as Tony Blair preached. Whatever that meant to the masses. New ways of spinning and manipulation were rolled out to present the holy message. Labour's political ethics colour in my opinion was not white, not even a whiter shade of pale as the song goes but more of a murky grey with black frayed edging.

I was to engage in an uphill battle to encourage higher values of public service and integrity into the soul of the party, politicians and Parliament. I would listen in amazement to one influential Labour official, a regional secretary, responsible for over sixty North West Labour MPs tell me that *if we allowed democracy into the* (Business) *forum they would go off on a tangent and we couldn't then control them*. I was perhaps from his point of few foolish to suggest democratic election of the executive council of a Labour party regional business networking forum.

2

GOING INTO LABOUR

Going into Labour wasn't too painful a process as newborn Labour was emerging, rosy cheeked and weighing in a lot healthier than the brotherhood of the loony left days. The days of militant politics were now memories for cities like Liverpool, London and beyond. New policies, new faces following a political makeover. Now wooing big business to counter-balance trade union purse-string influence. My belief that we all had a role for positive change on this planet drove me forward and was the fuel in the engine of my life. Politics was the vehicle to drive that change forward, but, as with any vehicle, parts wear out and drivers experience bumps and crashes. I have always believed that we all have access to networks of change within a worldwide network that provides opportunities for us to contribute for the common good.

A network that takes many forms including politics where effectively a positive charged ripple effect could come into play. As with many groups in society, even with community or charitable aims some participants waste time engaged in tribal warfare, many with self- interest agendas. Conflict with other networkers, with opposing factions emerging and self-interest agendas is perhaps an inherent human trait in tribal nature. Along the way the beneficiaries and people represented are sometimes forgotten.

The catalyst for my entry into the political world was the privatisation by stealth of the NHS by John Major's 1990s Conservative Government and issues around my mother's death on discharge from hospital. I was later in politics to be influenced by my mother's way of life as well as the manner of her death.

She was always a fighter, poor in material goods but rich in principle and integrity with a kind heart and support for many in the community, always there with a helping hand outstretched without strings attached to those in need. When I and others were made redundant at English Electric Co, Liverpool after finishing our engineering apprenticeships she took the redundancy issue up with local Labour MP, Simon Mahon. He was Member for dock- side Constituency Bootle near Liverpool. The MP's letter, which I still have, basically said there was nothing that he could do when the big boys eg the company owners made their decisions. Well at least Mam tried. I was twenty-one then and unaware she had written to the MP but she was still looking after her boys even though we had allegedly grown up.

The mismanagement of the NHS as well as creeping privatisation/PFI introduced by the Conservative administration pre-1997 was radicalising me. I had experience of working across many departments and services in the NHS during my business consultancy career. This had ranged from appraising hospital wide patient computer/management systems, improving procedures for the benefit of the newborn at a large maternity hospital, to working with pathologists and mortuary staff at the other end of the life cycle. I admit with guilt to always washing my hands rather quickly after shaking hands with the mortuary staff !

On the face of it, it seemed reasonable that the new Conservative approach of managing the NHS in the nineties was founded on principles of sound business methods of value for money. That seemed sensible but major flaws were to emerge with negative consequences. One policy introduced was the Resource Management Initiative. The initiative was based on

48

hospitals being split into individual Directorates with semi-autonomous Directors and managers responsible for budgets and planning for say General Medicine Directorate or Accident & Emergency Directorate. Millions of taxpayer monies were invested in the initiative, which sadly took clinical staff away from patient care and put in place more administrators and pen pushers. This initiative resulted in local hospitals not co-operating with each other. As a result hospitals started to compete against each other for so called customers and income streams. They also became reluctant to share innovation.

The move away from co-operation on such things as best practice and computer systems development was created by the internal market and competitive ethos by setting one hospital against another to win patients and funding. Privatisation by the back door rolls along still to this day, albeit with a different party mix in power. This was a policy, years later to be expanded with the Labour strategy of rolling out the private finance initiative so vehemently criticised by Labour when they were in opposition. A policy where the private sector seeks to become king in the NHS and the rise of the bureaucrats goes on unabated with un-elected/unaccountable quangos spending £billions of public money.

A UNISON trade union survey found that nine out of ten voters did not want private business to run public services yet politicians in government continue to ignore the democratic will of the people. The impact of politics affecting all our lives came home to me when my mother was admitted to a large local NHS trust hospital in October 1994 with chest pains and was kept in overnight for observation. She was admitted at 4-30 pm that evening and discharged the following morning to home where she lived on her own.

When I became aware of her intending discharge by a message from my sister I attempted to get hold of the ward doctor by telephone or paging system to prevent her discharge. I sent a fax to the ward with a copy to the Specialty Manager/Ward Manager and Staff Nurse expressing family concern about her discharge after only 22 hours in hospital. I stated that Mam's brother had died recently of a heart attack and we were seeking a diagnosis of Mam's condition and confirmation that she had had the full range of tests before she was to be discharged. I asked by fax four specific questions of the Clinicians including: Lastly but more important of all, we are seeking reassurance that her condition has stabilised to a level of safety and that her life is not at risk by her discharge.

I did not get a reply to that fax and Mam was discharged against the wishes of the family and died at home in the arms of my sister Jean days after her hospital discharge. Mam had succumbed to a massive heart attack. In the midst of my grief I sent a further fax to the ward two days later advising them of Mam's death. I said amongst other things the quick turn around of treatment will in no doubt feature in some future internal performance table of patient episodes.

I also wrote to the Chief Executive of the Trust a few months later with some searching questions and he replied some weeks later. One thing he did say was that Mam was not experiencing any pain and appeared happy to be going home. So that was all right then I presume from his reassurance, no pain, no stay, no investigation or appropriate treatment. He did also assure me that financial considerations played no part in the decision to discharge her.

In keeping with of our family's traditional political leaning during the autumn of 1994 I went to join the local Conservative Party near my home.

I met some very nice people but gained the impression that the party was not truly representative of a broad community profile. The local party consisted of mainly elderly females and mostly middle class members. No ethnic minorities, no disabled people either. I suppose I shouldn't have been surprised at that but that was the way things were at the time. Long serving Conservative stalwarts ruled the roost and would support the party come hell or high water even though the ship then was heading for a massive iceberg. I quickly discovered that in respect of the NHS the local members were completely out of touch as to the detrimental impacts the so-called Tory health initiatives were having on the health service. I attended a few local ward meetings and was encouraged to apply for selection as a local candidate in the forthcoming Council elections.

I was interviewed at home by a local businessman/party officer but was not selected to go forward. Perhaps I was too outspoken. Maybe I was too young or even too working class for them, being an ex-council house lad and son of a docker! At one meeting though a factional argument ensued with two groups disagreeing about policy or something. I cannot recall what the argument was about but as I was to find out within any volunteer organisations factions appear, squabbles are inherent and people fall out with one another. Consequently some people resigned and in their moment of madness somebody asked me to take the chair of the meetings.

Somewhat flattered as I was I was always very nervous about public speaking and lacked a lot of confidence after my 1992 heart attack and found it somewhat daunting. However I was determined to beat my fears and hid my panic and carried on. During my address to the Tory troops around me (all seven of them) I again expressed concerns about the growing public perception about uncaring and arrogant Conservative policies and especially my pet subject - the decline of the NHS. Yet again I got the impression that some were sadly out of touch, or possibly cocooned in a middle class retirement zone, which excluded some of the reality out there at the coal-face of public services. At one point looking ahead to the next general election in 1997 I made the analogy that the party was like the band on the deck of the Titanic and that disaster was looming for the party if they stayed on the same course.

That went down like a lead balloon and they looked at me like I was some sort of heretic. I was later proved right as events played out and New Labour election songs were broadcast heralding a new direction in politics and promising that things *can only get better*. My brief encounter with the Tory's ended after that, although thinking that Mam and Dad would not approve from their vantage point above of leaving the party of family choice. However it was a course I had to take. Some time after my short-lived taster with the Tory Party, who seemed to lack the vision for a better world I hopped on another political vehicle - the New Labour Express.

Like a modern train well presented, fast but tending to tilt on the many bends along the way, hindered by sleaze-like leaves on the line and political storms battering the route. I had difficulty making contact with local Constituency Labour so I phoned the local town hall and made an appointment to see the leader of the local Labour group of Councillors who was a dockland Bootle Councillor.

I was invited into his office and there was another senior Labour Councillor waiting to see me. Putting it nicely their welcome was cold to say the least and perhaps my suit and tie appearance frightened them. I was open with them and told them about my brief fling with the Conservatives and they were not too impressed. I explained about Mam's treatment in the NHS and my wish for a better health service etc but their eyes clouded over and they displayed not an ounce of compassion or sense of social justice between them during our meeting. The Labour Leader made a sarcastic remark to me asking me to think about joining the Liberal Democrat Party. At that point I decided to leave the local powerhouse of social justice and decided that they were not my kind of people. I was to cross swords with them in the future. Since then the Leader has passed away and the other one, for reasons known to himself and others, has vacated high office.

I had immense difficulty finding how to join the Labour Party and how to participate in local party activities and after some effort managed to join and attend the local Ward and Constituency meetings in Southport near Liverpool. There was no welcome or induction process for new members. The local party seemed to be a bastion of old Labour and I felt like a duck in a desert without rain. I supposed they considered me as a champagne socialist even though I was working class and the son of a docker and pub cleaner. I was treated even more like a heretic when I started to offer support to Tony Blair's new way forward. I turned up once unshaven and wearing jeans but that didn't impress them either.

Local efforts on political campaigning were a waste of time anyway as hell would freeze before Labour would ever be elected in that particular Constituency. The process of attempting to integrate as member of the Constituency team and gaining awareness of procedures and policies was abysmal and I decided to write the experience up as a new member case study. I sent the bound case study with recommendations from local to national level to Labour Party Head Office. I was subsequently invited down to London to give a presentation to the General Secretary, Tom Sawyer in December 1995.

My brief was to present my proposal on how it could be introduced to a large scale voluntary organisation encompassing 360,000 members in branches in rural and city areas with a multi-talented, mostly well educated membership - wow I thought. For support I invited my twin brother along as he, amongst other talents, was an expert on organisational development. As we were allegedly identical, he could be blamed by me for any cock-ups along the way. Sods law came into play and I got held up in the London tube system arriving at the Walworth Road Labour HQ an hour late and somewhat hot and bothered. The presentation went reasonably well although I was pretty nervous.

There was I, someone who had failed his eleven-plus, advising a major political party and senior management team on how to develop its people to win the next general election and get Tony Blair into power. Remarkably there was general agreement that the project should be implemented on a national basis. The Party subsequently had an offer of free consultancy from a company to support the project and one benefit amongst many was that the Labour Party became the first political party to achieve the National Investors In People award. My brother and I concentrated our voluntary efforts in the North West with input into the national programme across many different areas of development.

During the presentation to the General Secretary I suggested that as a party of social values and social justice Labour should consider integrating alongside the general party development a project I named as LIFT.

54

That stood for Labour Initiative For Transformation - for the community. The principle was that a data-base and structure of community volunteers be established from ward up to national level. This would consist of Labour Party members who would register their contact details, skills, experience and availability for volunteering in their local community. The message was that a caring political party would show that they practised what they preached on social matters by making available multi-skilled party volunteers to donate time, services, advice, materials or expertise etc for the common good.

One spin-off benefit of this would be a database the party could use for linking skills with campaigning needs during elections etc. On a community level the ultimate aim was tens of thousands of people hours made available to help others. The other spin-off was excellent public relations/media stories of New Labour in action supporting those in need in the community. The LIFT proposal was regretfully never taken up by the party of social justice with no reasons given. The concept however still remains valid to this day for any political party or membership organisation. Some years later I suggested a similar proposal to senior figures in the Conservative party who promptly binned the idea. So much for the much publicised *Big Society* principles and policy of the Conservative and coalition government.

Some weeks after the Labour party presentation I was asked by an up-and-coming official of North West Regional Labour Party to meet him regarding my developmental ideas. His name was David Evans and I subsequently became his unpaid mentor or David's *guru* as his staff described me. I met him at the North West Regional Office and from that day provided wide-ranging advice and support for the cause - all unpaid. I

55

provided occasional advice by phone and on-site on team building, people planning, fund-raising and election planning.

David was eventually promoted to Regional Director responsible for sixty odd Labour MPs/MEPs etc and the conduct and organisation of the party down to constituency level. Later on he became Assistant General Secretary in London and his colleague Andy Rowe, whom I also mentored, became special advisor to the First Minister in Scotland. Andy was close to the Blairs and John Prescott and had a good reputation in the party. Andy now has a well respected commercial PR company and is in great demand for his services across the UK.

I also worked with Jon Egan who was a key strategist in the team and a man of great intellect who later established his own PR/Media company - Aurora - in Liverpool. At that time a senior insider and leading force in the north west party was Frank McKenna who was and is very sharp, charismatic, entrepreneurial and well respected. He was a man of great vision and went on to form his own business ventures around the Downtown In Business brand in the north west, which went from success to success. As a business networking concept it is a market leader and links with business, community and across the spectrum of local and national politics. It is an ideal conduit to link the business sector with political decision makers.

The main aim of the regional office team 1995-96 was to manage and develop the resources for the target key seats in the 1997 general election and beyond. My role was to assist in building the team, to develop a clear plan of their key objectives, establish commitment to the plan, develop the team and resources and evaluate progress. This involved attending meetings and away days with the team. I introduced surveys and consultation with the customers of the regional office eg: the MPs/Shadow Ministers, their teams, Constituency Officers and union representatives and other stakeholders.

I was invited to a prestigious business dinner at the Granada TV Coronation Street set in Manchester in September 1996. Tony Blair as Leader and John Prescott, Deputy Leader were guest speakers. I shared a table with prospective MP Lindsay Hoyle and business and union guests etc. Whilst networking and chatting to people I noticed Tony Blair was shadowed by a blonde lady - Anji Hunter who was his PA or something like that. Some Regional Labour Party Officers had nicknamed her *Darth Vadar* for some strange reason. I said hello to the great man Blair, of future star wars celebrity status, that night and other political figures. Some perhaps where from Uranus I thought. That does need some thinking about.

As a fund-raiser various auction prizes were offered during the event to the gathered audience. The star prize was the offer of drinks and lunch with Tony Blair and John Prescott. The prize was to be taken at Westminster and I understood it was for two guests. I telephoned my brother who offered to help fund the auction bid. Part of me as a loyal disciple then was to have the benefit of a reasonable amount of time to talk with the two political celebrities and part of me wanted to build up the bid amount to the highest level and withdraw at the crucial moment. However I, by accident, turned out to be the highest bidder, won the auction bid and received an invoice from the Labour Party office the following week.

The cheque I paid them turned out to gather dust in someone's desk drawer for months afterwards and when they presented it to the bank it bounced. I hadn't checked my bank statement and presumed the cheque had been presented many weeks or months before. My wife and I had spent the money on other things. That was quite embarrassing and when they told me I quickly apologised and promptly paid. I thought party guru bounces cheque - yuk and was very concerned about my reputation. The amount eventually contributed was generous when we donated additional monies/ new telephone answering machine, services etc to the regional office. Cash and goods for access, but I never did get what was promised.

As it transpired after donating the monies I never had the pleasure of the prize I bid for. Weeks and months went by and no effort was made to contact me to arrange the trip for lunch and drinks with the dynamic duo in Westminster. I discovered later from a senior party source that some of the other auction prizes were allegedly not honoured for other bidders at that dinner. Perhaps I should have taken the event organisers or the Labour Party to court to obtain the promised auction prize or at least got my money back. As it transpired as part of my role I continued to be invited to other high profile events, dinners etc with politicians including Blair and Prescott but never did have the quality time lunch and drinks with Tony and John as the auction prize was detailed in the invoice.

Around that time I telephoned the Labour organiser of the party's prestigious national *one thousand club* and respectfully pointed out that with the auction monies/services etc I was entitled to become a thousand club member. They couldn't see my logic, ignored the substantial time, out of pocket expenses incurred by me in the national support I was giving and effectively told me to piss off. New Labour, new values. I was some years later to inform Cherie Blair about the breach of trust over the Blair/Prescott lunch offer but she chose as one does in high places to ignore the issue completely. The policy of building bridges around income streams with the business community was a New Labour priority. The party was very keen to generate political endorsement from the corporate sector as well as gain new sources of financial input in sponsorship and donations etc.

One of the things I did help support was a refurbishment of the regional office and sponsorship sourcing to make ready for the general election. John Prescott came to open the re-launched office. He did not have the need to punch me in the face I am pleased to say nor did he offer me the auction lunch and drinks but he was very pleasant with me. I think my blonde wig helped. During my time as a disciple/volunteer I met many MPs including Ian McCartney, later Government Minister who was for some years in charge of election planning and resources. He managed various important by-elections and campaigns. In a moment of madness I agreed to stand in the local Council elections as Labour Party Candidate in my own ward - albeit an unwinnable seat. The party chose me and another two candidates for the ward election. However the trio of photographs on the election leaflets would have scared anyone off. The female looked unhappy as if she had a chip or two on her shoulder.

The other male looked like a space traveller and in my photo I had a smarmy expression on my face. I was the official election agent for all three candidates and responsible for complying with electoral law. During the campaign that followed I had cause for concern. The legal requirements were very precise about submitting receipts etc for all election expenses to the Council Returning Officer at the election end.

Failure to comply with the election requirements was a criminal offence and I was very conscious about my responsibilities. During the campaign the agent is responsible for the control of the expenses within the legal limits and ensuring that what is printed on the leaflets is truthful and not defamatory. It was a legal responsibility to have my own name and address as the agent in an imprint printed on each election leaflet during the campaign. I soon discovered that although the ward election was supposedly targeted on local issues the content of the leaflets was pretty well imposed by other party members/councillors etc. They all lived out of the ward area. In particular some of the content on leaflets already printed, but not seen by me, was in my view inappropriate.

As a layman some of the wording seemed to me to be potentially defamatory to others and effectively endorsed in my name, which was printed on the bottom of the leaflet. I sought a second opinion from the party regional office and an official there shared my concerns. It was also alleged by a party insider that some of the leaflets and leaflets of other candidates were printed on the Council photocopier using Council paper. These were allegedly printed on reams of A4 paper intended for official Council use and certainly not for illegally subsidising political parties.

My difficulty also as the Agent was that I had to provide receipts for all printing and other allowable costs for the election. I felt I had no control as the so-called election agent and had no wish to be controlled by strangers who did not share my belief on how the campaign should be managed within the law. I again contacted the party regional office and spoke to the most senior person available who told me not to worry as, quote: *we can get you receipts*. New Labour - new ways of addressing electoral law? I promptly wrote to all relevant party officers by recorded delivery post and asked for assurances and genuine receipts etc. I wasn't at all comfortable with the election approach and consequently resigned as agent part way through the election. I insisted that all the leaflets in question were taken out of circulation and they were destroyed.

The ward seat went to the Conservatives, whom I am sure would have not been challenged with the problems I had. One successful initiative with the Labour Party team, which I helped develop, was to launch a regional business forum. I was invited to be forum council board member with the Regional Director and the great and the good of North West Labour and some of their corporate sponsors. This idea fitted in with the New Labour approach of wooing big business and reducing independence on the Unions. The new forum was later supported by a rich entrepreneur who funded the administration costs and provided links to big business in the region. The forum was called North West In Business and I was at its launch. The launch was held in Manchester in the trendy new Malmaison boutique hotel venue, with the media and big business in attendance.

A Government Minister was guest speaker. I was interviewed during the event and as recent media stories then speculated about alleged cash for questions by some MPs I made a linked joke to the eminent throng. I had prior to the launch been in the back seat of a car with a female Government Minister. Innocent situation of course, but during the interview I said I had had access to the Minister in the back of the car without cash changing hands or words to that effect. I meant it as a joke and to take the piss a bit but someone without a Liverpool sense of humour had later written it up in a party news publication as an inadvertent slip I had made. Their mistake or a bit of spin aimed at me perhaps for the unappreciated humour in front of influential people.

For me going into Labour and beyond was a political journey into, at times a vicious world where I would be aggressively challenged, defamed even, experiencing middle of the night phone call abuse at my family and more. On the positive side I met, idealism, integrity and was inspired by the example and support of good people of who wanted higher standards in public life and a better world for us all. Along the way there were of course many principled politicians doing good work, tirelessly working to serve the people rather than the party and self-interest but they sadly seemed to be subsumed by the many.

Perhaps my actual experiences in politics may only reflect society as a whole, but members of the public are not elevated in status and wealth and described as Honourable Members on a day to day basis. Going into Labour was for me a journey of insight into multi-faceted human nature. A political spectrum ranging from pure white to dark influences. Strong red politics pitted against blue and orange. Green fighting for influence with political colours now blending as policy switching sought out the black cross on the ballot paper. For some politicians it was a yellow brick road journey leading to power, fortune and influence.

To others it was a journey of disillusionment, loss of office and political frustration for many principled MPs. Many from the back-benches who sought a better way forward still were the vocal conscience of Parliament. The yellow brick road for many MPs led to well paid part-time jobs, consultancies and related financial benefits. The argument presented for MPs taking on those roles was for the experience it would give them.

Yet every sector in the business world and the not for profit sector has experienced and highly talented people, networks and resources to provide innovation, facts and policies for MPs to consider and consult on. Years later I was surprised to hear that the ex Chairman of the Labour Party/Seasoned Cabinet member, Ian McCartney MP, whose stationery once described him as socialist, had taken up a part- time advisory role for a major US company Fluor Corporation, one of the world's largest, publicly owned engineering, procurement, construction, and maintenance services companies. I anticipated that his reported remuneration of £115,000 would be put to good use in the spirit of the socialist philosophy.

I was to get frustrated by some cross party politicians hungry for control at any cost with some eager to jump on the gravy train of freebies, Directorships, Consultancies and fees for themselves and family resulting from their public service role. Aside from those MPs seeking supplementary private earnings the chipping away of democratic principles in the party and country by New Labour control barons, was of concern. Where power was God and traditional values and hard won rights excess baggage to be discarded in the Thames. Some freedoms and democratic rights washed away by a tidal swell of men and women with ambitions and personal gain taking precedence over public service and the defence of democracy. A decline in democracy, a loss of hard won freedoms with negative political actions unchallenged by on message MPs and a muted and falling party membership.

A largely apathetic or frustrated electorate were turned off by politics and despaired at having no real voice in the democratic process. An electorate for ten years or more living in reasonable economic prosperity as judged by the increasing sizes of their TV screens and frequency of holidays abroad. A decade of a feel good factor in the economy, the mission and Holy grail sought by all political parties. A sound economy allegedly in place largely due to the foundations laid by the Conservative economic policies and plain economic good luck. An economy in 2008 showed signs of unravelling as the honeymoon decade or so of prosperity was coming to an end. I was to admire the great intelligence, the acting skills, the mastery of words of some politicians, many legally trained but some lacking in common sense. Some ignorant of the real world and often lacking in passion or integrity in their elected responsibility to be servants of the people. I was to meet many high profile political figures and be impressed by some and shudder at the arrogance and apparent lack of soul of others. I believed I saw human nature at its best and worst, more so in the political system rather than any other sector of society.

Albeit some seeking power to change the world for the better with others seeking ways to change their own standard of life for the better. How I got involved was as they say an accident waiting to happen or fate - who knows? I believed I had a role to play in my life and politics was one element of that life mission for the greater good. Over the years I attempted to encourage policy regime change of direction in Downing Street via Blair's bed-mate, Cherie, with many proposals and ideas but the lady and he was not for turning. Well maybe he was only for turning away from socialist principles perhaps. The Prime Minister once said something like *forward, not back*. Taking tough macho decisions but driving forward his political career along a dark valley.

The *purer than pure* political pledge announced to the world with the oratory skill of a statesman, the performance of a world stage Oscar awarded actor. Pledges as yet undelivered, a dark force of Westminster sleaze and self-interest continuing to stain the corridors of Parliament to bring fresh ridicule on Prime Minister Brown, some in his team and politicians in general. Politics tarnished by the storm clouds of political sleaze in revelations emerging almost on a seasonal basis. New Labour, new scandals. Tory MPs maximising family income as well. More of the same from the servants of the people. When will they ever learn? Regarding Blair's Premiership I was to tell Mrs Blair that her husband *may be considered perhaps a good Prime Minister but would lose the opportunity to be remembered as a great Prime Minister if continuing on his course.* I also pointed out to her that this Government *could not organise a drinks party in a brewery* - she got the message. I got her answer back 15 minutes later.

She was very polite and focused on the Blair success story and was sad to hear of my disillusionment. That lady was indeed not for turning and she was later to disappoint me over a non political issue some years later. Working with the party I was to witness sophisticated political control by New Labour, new policies to the right of the party they had vehemently opposed for eighteen years. Policies badged as innovative uplifted from the Conservative Party, taken up and now promoted as the best thing since sliced bread.

In disbelief I saw a once proud political party born out of social justice values alienating many including disabled members of our community. Shocked and angry to the point that some outraged citizens in wheelchairs gathered outside Downing Street and a red paint protest ran like blood on the street. This was years later in 2005 when many were chilled to see Blair's proposed policy as the brother's keeper in a proposed but not implemented offensive against sick and disabled people. Perhaps history will be repeated when real blood will spill outside Downing Street as protests are mounted against the savage cuts on benefits proposed by the 2010 coalition government.

The Labour government plans, which were eventually shelved, were to means test families incomes and issue vouchers instead of benefits thus stigmatising the whole family because of illness and disability. Some years before I listened to a Labour Party Officer joke about rolling disabled people in their wheelchairs into Liverpool's Albert Dock as the disabled protested outside the dock side building visited by a Health Minister, Frank Dobson. I was to ask the Health Minister at a private audience there if the Government would consider putting more public money into hospice care in this country. His muffled reply, which is etched into my mind, was that *hospices do very well at fund-raising - they don't need our money*.

Children's hospices then were only getting about £6 in every £100 from Government sources. New Labour, New values. Frank had his chances then as a Minister but I can't remember what he achieved in the NHS or for the hospice care movement. He later went on to be somewhat outspoken and often rebellious even after leaving his ministerial role. I wasn't too impressed however with his attitude towards public funding for the care of the dying. I suppose the monies were needed for the welfare of struggling MPs.

I worked for a short time as a volunteer adviser and gained friendship with Martin Bell OBE, the ex MP and man in the white suit who wrote a book called *An Accidental MP*. In a way I suppose I accidentally got sucked into politics as a result of a personal tragedy. But perhaps in our lives accidents do not occur and the plot and script is already set in stone by a greater power than us lowly mortals. My Mother's death was my catalyst, the driving force taking me on the first steps of the political journey. A journey into politics that some people take with a wish to change the world for the better. I was in search of influence, to make positive changes for the common good, to try even though many had failed or lost their values and vision along the way. To engage rather than be an armchair critic and be critically constructive rather than complaining but not doing anything positive. To put money and effort where one's mouth was. I was perhaps over confident in some ways thinking that one person could affect powerful positive change as countless others had set out to before. As for me, who probably will never be judged as a great man or great achiever, history has shown that one man, one woman can make a difference in this world.

One person can achieve great things, touch countless lives with their life mission. The resultant ripple effect can reach out to different people and different parts of the globe. In my opinion the American web-site *http://thewayoftheheart.com* provides insight into life's mission and is something that perhaps politicians in particular and people in general should consider when they are alone with their thoughts. I referred Cherie Blair to it but whether she visited the web-site I will never know.

My stage of the life mission journey into politics was to take me and my family into a new world of politicians and would-be politicians, many self-serving, many scrambling up the greasy pole for power, glory and money. Last time I looked there was no job description for individuals holding public office as an MP. But for some politicians perhaps the job description could read: Must be willing to use people, bleed them dry, discard those people and move on to the next victim, must be willing to use power and office when personal needs dictate, must be a good actor and convincing even if you don't believe a word you are saying, especially if what you are promoting or defending is alien to your principles. Must also be prepared to be totally obedient to the party machinery in the interest of personal gain or career advancement. Adeptness and skill is required at not answering the questions put to you. You should also be content to put political party first before the democratic will of the Constituents who elected you etc. Such fine qualities of that reflective job description seemed to me to be part of the profile of some in politics.

However outstanding MPs and public servants of principle and integrity fighting their corner do continue to inspire hope. They know who they are and their Constituents do also. A breath of fresh air blowing through the musty corridors of the alleged Mother of all Parliaments. A challenge to those who brought politics into disrepute before and during the MPs' expenses scandal of 2009.

3

WHITE POLITICS

The birth of New Labour was for most people, including myself, then a joy to behold for many reasons. New people focused politics, new standards in public life and a caring party preaching social justice. The pledges and promises made were music to my ears and countless others across the nation. Untarnished, bright and shiny politicians travelled like white knights across the kingdom. They told the gathered people they would slay the political sleaze dragon and bring power to the people. The people now described as stakeholders by the party spin-doctors via the PR public address systems of Blair and Co Ltd. The promise was to deliver integrity and public service values to our society whilst working for the many - not the few. But behind the scenes, quietly toiling at the grimy coal-face of the political machine dark forces were at work. For some it seemed that nothing could stand in the way of achieving political victory.

As a smokescreen of white politics a new silky image of political purity was spun like a white cloak hiding the dark reality underneath. The weave and the spin of the fabric of new politics was pursued by servants of the political masters who aimed to please. Hidden from the light of day was a readiness by some, when needs must, to meet whatever price was needed to win and retain power. From 1995 to 1997 the Labour Party won me over and crucially the middle and working class vote by modernising their offer and attacking the Tories over alleged sleaze. The Sunday Times newspaper first broke the alleged cash for questions political scandal in July 1994 exposing how allegedly some politicians were willing to ask Parliamentary questions in exchange for payments.

The Conservative Party was vehemently attacked by the newly elected Labour Leader Blair, attacked for the sleaze and being the party of big business and self-interest. In the years to follow I would witness the new and blatantly hypocritical Labour strategy to woo those same big businesses and many more as allies for power. I failed trying to secure a party policy to engage with and value the small businesses who made up 99.7% of all UK businesses. Small businesses created the most jobs in the economy, which was a crucial point that many Labour politicians seemed to overlook. Perhaps their theme tune for dealing with business people should have been *Hey big spender, spend a little time with me rather than things can only get better*....In the last Labour Party Conference before their 1997 landslide General Election success New Labour Leader Blair assured the party faithful about new standards for political parties.

However less than a year into power the Labour administration managed to provoke public suspicion and lose substantial ethical credibility. This was manifested by accepting and later returning a reported one £1 million donation from Bernie Ecclestone, the Formula One Tycoon. It was downhill from then on in terms of battered political credibility, doubtful standards and ongoing allegations with many substantiated sleaze allegations against Labour made in the media.

Prior to the 1997 General Election I was an occasional volunteer providing advice and support to the North West Regional Labour Party. I was asked by a Regional Director of the party to provide whatever time I could to develop his key seats team for the forthcoming election. I was also asked to help establish a new national business forum network to win the hearts, minds and donations etc of the business community. I started by advising them to set clear goals and targets. This was backed by ongoing evaluation/surveys etc and a plan to develop the team and volunteers using business standards and processes. The initiative was about introducing practical management techniques and certainly not rocket science as some at the time considered it to be. I was also asked to help plan and support a key by-election to win a Parliamentary seat. The election was the crucial test-bed of improved electoral campaign planning and delivery. The party choice of Prospective MP told me he was selected because his image and background were more Tory than Labour.

I spoke at length with the candidate and other members of the team in my role supporting and evaluating the strengths and weaknesses of the campaign. The candidate had only been a party member for ten months and technically not eligible to stand under the party rules. However in the new world under Blair he was effectively the only choice for the Constituency Labour Party. He seemed a nice guy and told me after the election that he was instructed to do what he was told and he admitted to me that he took no part in campaign strategy meetings during his own election campaign.

Members of the candidate's election team produced a very detailed daily candidate's diary, which was given to him the previous day and he followed the diary schedule and went where he was told and did what he was told. There was for example one diary slot listed between 9.00 am and 11.00 am for: Candidate free time - buying suit and ties for photo shoot. Image of course was vital for New Labour. He told me he found it amusing to be in a car with Tony Blair and to

71

see Tony apply hair spray to keep his hair under control. Slick hair, slick image. The same day that he was selected as prospective MP he was out campaigning.

He told me the campaign policies came in from London each day. The election campaign proved to be both memorable and revealing in many ways. I was part of the campaign team managed by a powerful Strategy Control Group including John Prescott MP, Deputy Leader of the party, Ian McCartney MP as Political Manager and David Hanson MP who went on to become Prime Minister Blair's aide. The election agent was responsible for compliance within legal spending limits. Since its creation as a Parliamentary Constituency the Constituency had always returned a Conservative MP. Massive resources were made available in the Constituency to mount the Labour campaign.

An election HQ was quickly established for the candidate in a vacant main road shop premises, which soon accommodated about forty desk positions with a conference/ meeting room to hold thirty or so seats. Equipment and resources was impressive with computer software to track potential voters against the electoral roll. Phone bank facilities were provided on and off-site to cold call the voters and get out the vote. Although there were legal limits to what could be spent on the by-election, money didn't seem to be a problem, which was a constant concern to some in the party. With an election war chest probably of such magnitude expenditure must have, or should have been sanctioned at the highest level in the party.

Tony Blair had visited the Constituency three times to support the candidate and numerous trips were made by other MPs to get out the voters. I also met Gordon Brown at the election centre and managed to have a one to one discussion about the massive waste of taxpayer money on doubtful NHS computer systems. He seemed very interested and asked me to send him some of my research and recommendations, which I did. Nothing came from that contact and information provided. It seems that the lessons were not learned by New Labour about NHS development failures under the Tories. The hundreds of £millions wasted then became tens of £billions wasted on failed computer systems and doubtful projects under Chancellor Brown's prudent financial management over the next decade. Each year it seemed reports were emerging about wasted public monies on failed computer systems. MPs in the Public Accounts Committee condemned as a shambles a major IT project aimed at tracking offenders through the criminal justice system. It was said that the system was abandoned two years before after costs trebled to £700 million. It was alleged that management was so poor that they had no idea what £161 million spent before October 2007 was used for.

It would be unbelievable in the private sector and why politicians and public servants fail to learn the lessons from the recent and not so recent past is a mystery. Accountability, commercial best practice and professional standards appear sadly lacking in many public spending projects. New Labour, new levels of failing to get value for money. Resources and monies diverted from front-line patient care and frittered away. Massive waste sanctioned when medicines and treatments were denied to sufferers and hospices were facing closure due to lack of public funds.

During the election campaign I also met future Culture/Olympics Minister, Tessa Jowell MP. I talked to her about ideas for a more cost effective and co-ordinated approach to business start and support by a New Labour Government. The proposed strategy was based on my twenty five year career providing business support from start-up to Plc level. Her pretty eyes glazed over quickly and that's about as far as that got. She was quite attractive in a political way but she was probably thinking Tessa meets Tosser. Years later as Olympics Minister the original Government estimate for the London Olympics was around £3 billion. This was later revised by Tessa in the Commons to £9 billion with independent opinion saying the final bill would be around £20 billion. New Labour, new excess costs taking money away from public services and good causes. Tessa's husband was an international corporate lawyer, years later to be spotlighted in the national media.

A key driving force in the by-election was Ian McCartney MP once described as Labour's *Pocket Battleship* and later influential DTI Government Minister, responsible for the minimum wage etc. Ian was in the top ten echelon of New Labour and was the driving force of campaign strategy in many other elections to follow. Following his appointment as Minister, the Spectator magazine awarded him with *the Minister to watch* accolade. His wife Ann worked for many years in the Bootle, near Liverpool, office of Bootle MP Joe Benton was a dedicated party activist. For years afterwards I would get a Christmas card from Ann and Ian until I distanced myself from the party.

During the night of the election and awaiting the count I was in the election centre and most people were out celebrating the anticipated victory for New Labour. On one desk unattended there was a large sum of banknotes, which I thought was a crazy practice in any office situation. I hid the money in the desk drawer and told the election administrator later on. Well it wasn't real money was it? It was meant to be spent. Consequently all the efforts of the MPs and team with the massive financial investment paid off. The candidate was elected by a large majority. Michael Crick, author and political correspondent for BBC 2 Newsnight programme, was investigating alleged overspend breaching electoral law and we were to meet a few times over the years. I was facing major health challenges in my life and did not want to be part of a planned media exposé against New Labour. Michael was a really nice guy and visited me at home and introduced me to some very interesting people and the Groucho Club in London. Newsnight, Jeremy Paxman, was later to send me his signed book *The English* and he wrote in it: *To Bill - I hear you have been plotting in my office.* I had actually been sitting in Jeremy's chair in his office.

The end result of victory at any price in that particular election did however show the country that New Labour could win the hearts and minds of so-called Middle England. The dragon of the loony left Labour Party image had been slain. Within days following the by-election the Labour Party made preparations to win the many more key seats in the North West and the rest of the UK. I suggested a debriefing team meeting to learn the lessons from the campaign and promote best practice. With help from the team I wrote up a paper on the campaign organisation as a benchmark for future elections. I was asked to be a speaker at a rallying key seats seminar for hundreds of party officers, volunteers and MPs, Shadow Ministers etc with dozens of prospective MPs.

At the time I was exhausted because of a debilitating long term illness and somewhat reluctant to participate. However, my conscience overcame my good sense and I agreed to go on the stage with the great and the good. When I did my presentation I felt most unwell with sleepless nights previously affecting my performance. I came across so badly I promised myself afterwards I would never speak in public again. I thought I was going to faint or worse and basically did not project my message well at all. The microphone and overhead projector failed and I just wanted to dig a big hole and hide from the delegates. The expression - he died on stage was quite appropriate. Well I suppose we are only human and that night I blew it. To make matters worse I had designed seminar evaluation sheets for feedback from the delegates and some criticism of my contribution came across when I analysed the responses. The moral of the story was follow your inner voice, which told me to say no to the invitation from the organisers. However one kindly senior union official spoke to me after my so-called speech and suggested that we meet to follow up some of my ideas. He for one seemed quite impressed. Sometime afterwards

I did move on from the ordeal and over the years overcame my fears and went on to speak again in public meetings, do karaoke songs in public and more. I even did a stand up comedy slot in front of a business audience in an event called *stand up and be counted* to raise money for charity. It was at the Albert Dock in Liverpool in a well known night club and bar. Although petrified I have always tried to face my fears as I did that night. We are all human and have our strengths and weaknesses.

Whilst doing my comedy act I got carried away and overran my ten-minute slot and they virtually had to drag me off stage. I didn't mind people being amused at my performance that night. Just before the 1997 General Election I was asked by a senior party manager to see what campaign support I could give to secure victory for Martin Bell, the man in the white suit who was standing as Independent candidate in the fourth safest Conservative seat in the country. The irony was that in theory a Labour Party member supporting a non-Labour Candidate would normally be expelled from the party. New Labour, new bendy rules, which set the scene over the next decade. The Labour aim was to take out the sitting Conservative MP of Tatton in Cheshire. In normal circumstances Tatton would probably never be a Labour seat. But the circumstances were anything but normal.

The sitting MP, Neil Hamilton, was ostracised by the media for alleged payments to him in brown envelopes by Mr Al Fayed of Harrods. Yet much later on in November 1997 the Committee on Standards in Parliament found that on a specific charge of receiving £20,000 in brown envelopes......*there can be no absolute proof that such payments were, or were not made*. Neil was caught up in the media frenzy of cash for questions against Conservative MPs who allegedly asked questions in the House of Commons on behalf of business donors, questions allegedly, which would be of commercial or personal interest to the donors. Neil was fighting to keep his seat and various independent candidates emerged from around the country to contest that seat.

There were ten candidates in all including Lord Byro - a poet, a theatrical attired seven foot transvestite called Miss Moneypenny whom I believed had a night club in the Midlands. Martin Bell as a BBC Reporter on the world stage was apparently asked by well connected Labour supporters and Tony Blair's guru, Alistair Campbell, to stand as a Independent to depose Neil Hamilton. After some initial reservations Martin agreed and consequently took early retirement from the BBC. Martin was well respected with high standards and was awarded an OBE in 1992. He was well-known as an international war reporter and famous for wearing a white suit at all times.

The New Labour strategists probably thought that the White Knight had indeed arrived. Martin was clearly a formidable challenger, a man of principle, a brave man who was wounded by shrapnel in 1993 whilst reporting with the BBC in war-torn Bosnia.

With Martin in the frame as the ideal choice the two main opposition parties had offered to stand down their own candidates. Paddy Ashdown from the Lib Dems had phoned Martin to offer his support. John Prescott MP, future Deputy Prime Minister with Ian McCartney MP, future Minister had travelled to the Constituency to address all the local Labour Party members to seek their approval to withdraw their candidate Jon Kelly. The vote was carried with a massive majority to drop the Labour challenge and support independent Mr Bell. It was said that both politicians gave passionate speeches of the need to withdraw the Labour candidate Jon Kelly. Jon was a really nice genuine person who became an asset to Martin and the team during the campaign.

Labour made arrangements and I travelled to Knutsford in Tatton, Cheshire to meet Martin shortly after he arrived in the Constituency. We had arranged to have a private chat in his hotel about Labour support and he took me up to his hotel bedroom. It was very surreal as we walked into his room there were three very attractive young women with Martin. He must have thought he was in heaven. I did anyway. Two ladies were outstretched on the bed - fully clothed of course. Martin ended up sitting on his bed with a beautiful lady besides him as we talked about the election campaign. Martin assumed I was the world's expert on running elections by the questions he was asking me and I could not disappoint him. He seemed satisfied with my responses anyway.

The three ladies had heard about Martin's mission to unseat Neil Hamilton and had contacted Martin to be volunteers in his campaign team. They were very intelligent, good looking, media experienced and proved to be a great asset in his campaign. The media were later to name the ladies, which included two sisters, Bell's Belles. Another member of the Belles was Martin's attractive daughter Melissa whom again had media experience with Reuters and was a very articulate and determined lady. An election centre was quickly established in a large vacant retail shop in the shopping centre of Knutsford, Cheshire. A senior national Labour Party organiser, Alan Olive was provided by National Labour HQ - Millbank for most of the election.

We set up an office base/war room in the back of the showroom. Martin, Alan and I had desks there and I used my home computer and printer to edit/prepare some of the election manifesto for Martin with other campaign documents. Martin was not computer literate then and relied on his trusty typewriter, which had seen more words of war than even Tony Blair had. Martin was quite flattering to me and would come in to talk and seek advice about aspects of the campaign and christened me his *guru*. He appeared to be generally happy with my suggestions and asked me if I would consider thinking about being his aide at Parliament after he won the election.

I said I would consider it, but it never happened as he didn't follow up his original proposal. Martin Bell was as a man described as having great integrity with over thirty two years media career. He clearly had many talents, with public speaking being his bread and butter but he had never been involved in an election campaign before. He was therefore directed to some extent by what his cross-party political support team were saying.

The pressure from Labour for him to stand as *anti-corruption candidate* was intense and I believe that is how his first set of election nomination papers where completed. The external pressure was also mounting on Martin and tabloid newspapers were attempting to dig for dirt on him because of what he stood for and his white suit image. It was alleged that the media were even looking through his dustbins and trying in vain to find personal skeletons in the cupboard to make a headline story. His second wife in America was contacted, his daughter also and others who knew Martin. Martin was however a man of high standards and they had nothing on him.

Martin was to face faxes and letters from Neil Hamilton's Solicitor, which left Martin in no doubt about legal redress if unsubstantiated allegations were presented from the Bell camp during the election campaign. At one point Martin spoke to me about his concerns regarding his legal position and responsibilities. He was extremely concerned about the legal pressures and tabloid press intrusions into the lives of his family and friends. On his registration for the election there was great doubt as to whether his description (Labour's preference) as *independent anti-corruption* candidate would be accepted by the electoral authorities on ballot papers. Two actions followed.

The first was that I telephoned Labour Party HQ, North West and eventually spoke to David Evans, Regional Secretary, and Shadow Minister, Ian McCartney MP about Martin's situation. I suggested quite forcefully that Martin should not be placed in this stressful legal minefield situation to meet a Labour strategy. I didn't want him to be left vulnerable and thrown to the wolves because he had no professional legal advice. After some consultation, Labour in conjunction with the Lib Dems agreed to provide the services of legal opinion for Martin's campaign. This was a great relief to me as I thought Martin should be valued for what he was doing and not used as a political pawn.

At that time during the frenzy of the campaign and long hours for Martin and others, there was no mention whatsoever of any legal cost implications for Martin. The assumption was that main parties supporters from the legal profession would provide their services as a favour. eg - pro bono. The second action was the dropping of the potentially defamatory candidate description. As the deadline to get the election papers in was the next morning the description on Martin's election application form was changed to Independent. Martin's proposers on the nomination paper was a local Conservative Councillor and the seconder was a former Labour Mayor for Knutsford. The former Liberal Democrat Mayor was also supporting Martin.

This was a cross-party support formula which was unique in British political election history. The election process for the nomination meant that a number of signatures from electors in the Constituency had to be found and found that night. Again it was surreal as late at night beyond midnight we travelled the Constituency visiting people's homes to obtain the required nomination signatures.

Some people were in pyjamas and ready for bed. I recall standing next to one lady in her home who was in a revealing nightdress whilst signatures were entered. The paperwork was thankfully submitted on time and a legal challenge was avoided. My unintended survey of the sleeping attire of residents of Cheshire came to a swift end. No more revealing female nightwear for me to assess or fluffy slippers to view. The dawn of the next day saw intense gearing up in readiness for the election. Amazingly world media attention was to be focussed on the small town of Knutsford in Cheshire over the next few weeks. I was to take calls from people like BBC reporter Jeremy Bowen from the Middle East, Kate Aide and others from Russia and beyond.

Martin Bell was to be *ambushed* by Neil and Christine Hamilton in front of the media with searching questions on Knutsford Heath. Martin was later to tell his story in his book An Accidental MP in 2000. What Martin as Independent candidate was unaware of though was undeclared party funding effectively subsidising his campaign that was not revealed to him or his election agent - Kate Jones. Independent Kate as a lady of high integrity and professionalism travelled to help Martin with his campaign for higher standards in public life and was not a member of the Labour Party. She was involved in book publishing and in a twist of fate some ten years or so in the future was to work with Cherie Blair on her book. Kate sadly died before Cherie's book was published and Cherie paid tribute to Kate in her book. Kate played a major role in Martin Bell's campaign but was as much in the dark as Martin was about undeclared campaign related funding.

Some years later a respected senior regional figure and high profile party activist was accused with a colleague of alleged participation in election return irregularities. The consequence was that the police mounted a dawn raid on the family homes to follow up that allegation. An alleged breach of electoral law, which clearly caused great concern and trauma to the families concerned. The case was eventually thrown out of court some time later with no case to answer and their reputations cleared. However the hypocrisy of the Labour Party in the knowledge of their election expense policies was that the two involved, who had suffered loss of positions etc were effectively treated as untouchables by some in the party. I was told by a party insider close to Blair, Prescott etc to keep away from those who were wrongly accused. I ignored his advice and was glad I offered support when many turned their backs on them.

4

WHITE SUIT IN THE DARK

The campaign to elect the man in the white suit started on Tuesday 8th April 1997. It took place in the affluent town of Knutsford, Cheshire, in the Parliamentary constituency of Tatton, the Constituency of the future Chancellor of the Exchequer - George Osborne. Some leading local Conservatives unhappy with Neil Hamilton standing again as MP joined forces with Labour and Liberal Democrat activists and others. This was an unprecedented cross-party/no-party alliance to unseat a servant of the people who was facing serious allegations. Hundreds of other volunteers previously politically inactive came forward to support the campaign. Concerned voters from around the UK, some even from abroad seeking higher standards in public life, flocked to the campaign or donated time, money or equipment.

I recall one night when I was in the Election Centre just before midnight there was a loud knock on the front door and a very large Scottish man in full highland attire including kilt and sporran turned up. I thought the Scottish Nationalist Party was attempting to get in on the act. The Scotsman said he had read about the campaign and wanted to help Martin become an MP. He told me he had come from either Loch Ness or Loch Lomond and I thought whoops is he for real. It was definitely surreal but the guy seemed genuine, albeit slightly eccentric perhaps and added interest to the midnight hour. He had a great accent. I didn't know whether to assign him to the front door as bouncer to keep strange people out, or to give him a job knocking on voters' doors. I can't remember exactly what happened to him as he seemed to slip back to the dark cold waters from whence he came. Some did think he could have been a Tory plant such was the election paranoia. I for one was not willing to check his sporran for hidden cameras or microphones. His solid hairy legs looked like dangerous weapons to me so I wouldn't go too near him.

The mix of people amongst the campaign volunteers and donors was amazing from millionaires and high profile professional people like Barristers to young children who donated pocket money. There was romance in the team also political intrigue represented by many things including one senior Lib Dem Official who admitted he had secretly taped a campaign-related discussion with others on the campaign. There were displays of human nature at its best and not so best. Political paranoia was rife and I ended up sleeping one night at the election centre for reasons of security. A female Vicar named Pauline Pullen, complete with white dog collar, and great dignity volunteered to help out. When she arrived I suggested she become our front of house receptionist as her image at the point of arrival in the centre would be good public relations. In Martin we hope but in God we trust, I thought. She did a brilliant job and went on to work with Martin in his Constituency office after the election. I also have one vivid memory of an elderly and distinguished looking couple turning up who looked like they were out shopping at ASDA. They arrived at the centre with a lot of office furniture etc for the campaign.

They looked like an ordinary retired couple but after chatting to them I discovered it was multi-millionaire John Moores Jnr and his wife Jane from the Littlewood's Pools, Chain Stores and Mail Order business empire. Ordinary people with extraordinary financial resources and social values who wanted to change the world for the better. Millionaires who were strong supporters and contributors to The Labour Party were now showing their support in a very practical manner with the essential items they delivered after an hour or so drive from Liverpool. I provided a wish list of equipment etc that was needed for the campaign and the Moores did their best to provide those items. Martin Bell told me he had received four figure sum donations by cheque from people like the Moores but had returned the cheques for policy reasons.

Martin had set a maximum limit of £100 per donation from people during the campaign for ethical reasons. The money kept flowing in accompanied by hundreds of letters of support. A middle aged lady arrived from Brussels and got allocated administrative tasks. She pinched my bottom once when passing and winked at me. But she wasn't my type and I was of course happily married. I later discovered her worse for drink whilst on campaign duty during the day in the election headquarters. Unrequited love perhaps? She was politely asked to go home and take a break. On another occasion an agitated member of Swampy's team with muddy boots turned up and virtually stormed the election centre.

I and others spoke to him to try to calm him down. Plans were underway to build another runway at Manchester Airport across the Cheshire green fields and woodlands. Swampy as he was known to the media led a team of supporters in the woods with people virtually living in tree tops on ropes, in burrows and huts to stop the building contractors. The eco-warriors had good intentions clearly and there was a lot of local support for their aims in preventing loss of green belt, opposing aircraft noise and fuel pollution. However the swampy man who turned up at the door of Martin's election centre was in my opinion a bit hostile as he was seeking an immediate statement from Martin to support the eco-warriors. He was very impatient and the message coming across from Swampy's camp was that Martin's election centre would be swamped with Swampy's protesting supporters unless endorsement was forthcoming. He was also dismayed that Martin had not visited their encampment in the midst of the woods. Luckily he calmed down before he chained himself to anything solid and good sense prevailed. He disappeared back into the woods amongst the greenery to be roped back into things. Perhaps he was a swing voter I thought.

Martin Bell sometimes described his campaign arrangements as the contraption and this probably stems from a volunteer Labour Party activist from the Midlands who joined the campaign team and left a few days afterwards in dismay. The short-lived Bell activist became frustrated with what he felt was the lack of direction and organisation in the campaign centre. He left the campaign and followed up with a critical letter about the Bell campaigners published in the Guardian newspaper. This was not very helpful but he was proved wrong in the end as the election result was to prove. After meeting him it came across strongly that he failed to understand that from scratch to organise logistics and deal with hundreds of would-be volunteers, letters, monies, resources, legal issues etc as well as deal with the media was a formidable time-consuming task.

If he had stayed on as a team member then he would have seen the *contraption* develop into a winning piece of election machinery that outperformed the opposing Conservative camp in every possible way. I suspected he wanted to lead rather than to be led, a Chief rather than an Indian, in the hierarchy but that option was not available to him at the time. Another notable volunteer who played an active part in the campaign was brave and straight talking soldier, war veteran future MP Colonel Bob Stewart who was a media figure well-known from the conflict in Bosnia. Ex Deputy Chief Constable of Manchester, John Stalker, actively supported Martin during the campaign. John again was like Bob Stewart a man of great integrity and both men added great value to the campaign. Actor/singer David Soul from the American Starsky and Hutch programme added glamour to the campaign and was a tireless worker supporting Martin.

Martin's nephew, Oliver Kamm, who appeared like the brain of Britain was Martin's personal adviser, which was clearly a change from his normal job in investment banking. The Press Officer was a very experienced journalist named Kate Edgley, who in conjunction with Martin's Election Agent Kate Jones, made a formidable twosome. The campaign was supported by volunteers from the legal profession including Anthony Crean, a Barrister whose good looks made women swoon, or so they said.

A Business Consultant named Nick Grant, and Sue Addison who was a pharmacist, both contributed much time, support and equipment during the campaign. Nick and Sue both went on in later years to form with me our think-tank called The Democracy Trust but that is another story. A Former BBC Producer, David Geen, was allocated the task of compiling Martin's daily itinerary into a Candidate's Diary. On most days Martin had interviews or press conferences with international media, TV, national newspapers and magazines like Time and the Spectator etc.

Diary man David Geen was good at his job role but tended on occasions not to share the diary with key colleagues. It is difficult to describe now, but as people were moving in and out of the campaign it produced a climate of mistrust to some degree. Any new volunteer seen to be making notes was seen as a potential Hamilton camp spy or a tabloid reporter looking for cracks in Martin's white halo. Another late volunteer to the team arrived from Labour HQ Millbank in London. His name was Peter Bracken and he was a former army Major working as a volunteer at the Labour Party's Millbank headquarters. He was a very handsome and talented guy but perhaps was not fully briefed before he left Millbank.

The message to Labour employee, Alan Olive the national campaigns' expert and I as Martin's back room boys was that our Labour Party influence should be played down. Martin had to be presented as a completely Independent Candidate. I in particular kept a very low profile and most of my work was at a desk in the war-room at the back of the election centre. Alan Olive kept well away from the media also. When Peter Bracken turned up he quickly made it clear in front of people that he was from Labour Party HQ to provide help. This openness was a little embarrassing and I had a polite word with him to ask him to keep his Millbank connection to himself. During a chat with Martin's daughter Melissa on the first day that Peter arrived I actually told her that she would marry him. Prophecy or coincidence perhaps I was later invited to their wedding and they made a lovely couple, later to make Martin Bell a grandfather. Interestingly enough in July 1997 there was a media story about the engagement of Peter to Martin Bell's daughter, Melissa.

The article mentioned Peter's volunteer role at Millbank and later with Martin Bell and quoted David Hill, the Labour Party's Chief Media Spokesman saying: *Millbank had not been formally involved, but had offered assistance...people did work for Martin Bell but it was not a formal involvement,* he allegedly said.

So it would seem that New Labour considered the provision of a paid employee - Alan Olive from Millbank, as not formal involvement, never mind the significant logistical support including legal advice, leaflet preparation and printing, cash purchases and so on. I wondered what resources would have been brought to bear if there was formal involvement by the Labour Party.

Whatever their origins the mix of people involved in the campaign was probably unique in political campaigning history. A melting pot of opposing political views, people from across society's spectrum, rich and poor, drunk and sober, good looking and otherwise coming together for one purpose to get a non-politician elected. Strange as it seems a quartet of the campaign team had a unique connection in their fight for higher standards and values in public life that the campaign was all about. The connection was that they all had a close call with their own mortality. Martin Bell was wounded and could have been killed in Bosnia.

His Election Agent, Kate Jones, was then bravely recovering from cancer surgery whilst working in the campaign. Sue Addison who was a tireless volunteer and donor to the campaign was recovering from a near fatal car road traffic accident with the scars still visible. Finally I myself had faced a life-threatening situation on five occasions prior to 1997 and had just about survived. I believe that fate sometimes brings people together for a purpose and perhaps this was such an occasion.

During the election the respected reporter John Sweeney from the Observer newspaper covered the campaign and although professionally neutral was very supportive of the Bell camp. He almost became almost one of the team as he seemed to be imbedded into the campaign for hours on end. John later went on to write a book called *Purple Homicide*, which in my opinion did not really reflect the heart of the campaign. John wrote to me and others in the campaign to source material for his book. I never did provide any material for him. John was later to find other fame of sorts when he was featured by the world media and on youtube. He was shown to the world as having lost his temper in what seemed to be an out of character public rant at supporters of the Scientologist Church in America during his investigative reporting on the church.

I sent him an email of support suggesting that we were all human and do things we later regret. I spoke to him briefly also with a potential news story and he promised to get back to me on returning from holiday. He never did keep that promise to contact me. World media attention on the Bell campaign from Europe to Australia was amazing as reporters came from across the globe to cover the story. Martin also had letters of support from Sir Alec Guinness and Michael Foot, ex Labour leader to name a few. However the Labour Party aim during the campaign was to play down the influence of Labour's support for Martin by keeping a low profile and it seemed to be the case of don't trust anybody for fear of Conservative infiltration.

Martin's campaign team and the back-up political resources were very skilled at PR and image building. The canvassing team wore white rosettes and the leaflets and posters were black and white print, described by some as a United Nations look. People were asked to display a white ribbon on lapels, on car aerials, on garden gates and trees etc. During the campaign a local Conservative had a display of a different kind. He displayed lots of brown envelopes stuck on the window of his stationery shop in Knutsford town centre. This was clearly to get the message across about the alleged cash for something issue, which drew so much media attention to the Tatton election. My daughter aged nine then and her friend came with my wife to visit and support me during the campaign. The children coloured their own little posters of support for Martin and stuck them to the election centre shop window.

The kids could see what a nice man Martin was. Years later I was to meet another nice man, Neil Hamilton with his wife, much quoted battleaxe Christine Hamilton and have tea with them at a posh boutique hotel in central London. I was struck by how honest and genuine they both were, which left me thinking that Neil was to some degree a scapegoat victim of hypocritical politics. I contacted them to talk to them about the book I intended to write and also to find out more about their availability for charitable events. I turned up for the meeting at a posh boutique hotel in central London in my best suit, shirt and tie. They turned up on bicycles, dressed very casually leaving me feeling very overdressed.

We had a really good meeting. I had my photograph taken with them in the hotel garden but it didn't turn out for some reason. Christine's Mum used to live not far from me in a market town called Ormskirk. Christine was later to kindly write to me with words of support to try to prevent a hospice being closed down in Ormskirk. Cherie Blair/Booth was described by the charity as Vice President of that hospice, which was eventually closed down. Another element of Tony Blair's legacy - lack of sufficient financial support for end of life care in England.

A few years later some of the multi-millions of earnings and potential earnings into the Blair bank accounts would have kept that hospice going until other income streams came on line. That would have been a great Blair legacy for posterity in keeping with the Christian faith. The Bell campaign rolled on and was taking its toll on all the participants, the long hours and countdown to election day affecting the campaign workers. Martin must have been exhausted but he didn't show it. I had a date booked for surgery straight after the election and was in a lot of pain and felt quite exhausted. I used to quietly disappear back to my hotel room for rest during the day and early evening, but such was the atmosphere and vibrancy around the campaign that I had to stick with the team until the election result.

Thanks to the cross-party resources ploughed in the quality of Martin's leaflets/election material was excellent and well researched and presented. The leaflets distributed overwhelmed the Conservative best efforts and many were printed in Liverpool or by Labour printing equipment. The banner headline for Martin was Trust-Honesty-Integrity. The leaflet contained polling data from the ICM poll, which forecast Martin gaining 50% of the vote and Neil 39%. There was also a summary of poll results on one leaflet showing that three out of four Constituents trust Martin Bell a great deal.

This was stated as the highest rating for any politician standing anywhere in the country. Less than flattering poll results were published on the leaflet about Neil Hamilton. On 17th April 1997 Martin Bell actually wrote to the then Prime Minister, John Major, asking for a meeting. On 30th April, Martin got a reply, which basically said that Neil Hamilton was entitled to a fair hearing before being judged and that the Prime Minister in the middle of an election campaign could not meet candidates opposed to those he supported.

The day of the election came and we were invited to attend the count at Macclesfield Leisure Centre. I got there after midnight and Martin and his daughter

Melissa arrived about 1.00 am in the morning. As Martin walked into the counting room it was amazing as the majority of ballot paper counters rose to their feet and applauded Martin. Yet again surreal, but witnessed by the waiting world media lined up on the balcony above. Unique perhaps as an event unseen before in British electoral history. Martin went on to win the Parliamentary seat with 29,354 to Neil's 18,277 votes cast.

The campaign team and Martin went back to party most of the night at a hall in Knutsford. Donors had contributed lots of food and drink and many bottles of champagne and we had the mother of all celebrations. I had brought from home a large brass bell salvaged from a bombed out church in Liverpool perhaps decades before, which I polished and I gave to Martin that night as a souvenir of the campaign. I spotted the bell in Martin's home during a televised interview he had some years later. The party was waning as exhausted campaigners drunk with victory and much more went home to their homes or hotels. My wife and I left to stroll with T.V. star David Soul and an armful of bottles of champagne, which were party left-overs.

We crossed the dewy Knutsford Heath and said goodbye to Starsky or was it Hutch and his lady friend to fit in about two hours of sleep. We awoke with headaches to a new Labour Government in power with Martin as the first Independent MP for decades amongst 658 other MPs. We joined Martin in Knutsford town for a walk about with the world's media and we nursed sore heads compensated with happy hearts. We helped with de-commissioning the election centre and I was passed an official expense claim form from the Labour Party to reclaim my-out-of pocket expenses. Labour Minister Ian McCartney's wife Ann from her Labour Party MPs office in Bootle provided lots of advice and documentation to me to help Martin settle into his role as Constituency MP. Martin kindly wrote to me later and said:

Dear Bill. To have done what we did and win a famous victory in so short a time was no less than a political miracle. It was a miracle that you made happen. I think that it is something we can all be justifiably proud of. I am certainly proud of you and will never forget what you did. Our election 'contraption' will be the envy of campaigns in other elections for years. Thank you for being part of it and a very special part. My thanks to your family for enduring your absence.

We were later invited to Martin's so-called party conference some time later on a local farm near Knutsford. But as Martin pointed out you just can't have a party of Independents as it would be like having a convention for hermits who just want to live solitary lives. During the party I managed to capture a photograph of Martin standing next to me with a large brown envelope in his hand. I think he forgot about the significance of the envelope but I thought it was quite amusing. I didn't send a copy of it to the Private Eye magazine. I was later to visit Tatton quite frequently and on May 21st 2001 met the then prospective Tory MP George Osborne in a Question Time type debate organised by the local Knutsford Guardian. I was invited by the newspaper in my capacity as founder of The Democracy Trust to chair the meeting of all the prospective candidates in the forthcoming General Election. It was a public meeting and I was very nervous but it seemed to go off ok. Strangely one of the candidates that night had a white suit on, but it wasn't Martin Bell.

The Democracy Trust had produced a twelve-point citizen focussed code of conduct for MPs and prospective MPs to endorse, which seemed fair and reasonable to the overwhelming majority of people who read it. Some of the candidates that night signed it and I believe George Osborne said he agreed with its principles. Mr Osborne went on to take Martin Bell's Tatton seat when Martin Bell stood down. As Shadow Chancellor later on he enjoyed a fast-track record of senior positions in the Conservative hierarchy. George Osborne with a high media profile seems to have a done extremely well. On the night of the debate he came across as the most competent candidate and seemed to be a very genuine person.

I kept in touch with Martin over the following years and he bought me a drink in the House of Commons bar amongst other things - much to the dismay of some Labour members who were giving me funny looks. Martin went on to represent what he was elected for - a principled politician who genuinely believed in high democratic standards. Thirteen years later he was still sought by the media for his opinions on standards in public life. Past and current issues of public concern like the gravy train that some MPs seem to indulge in with snouts in troughs when some of their constituents they represent are in poverty or despair.

Martin as MP went on to offend the Labour Government when he asked a Parliamentary question of Prime Minister Blair about the alleged one million pounds given by Bernie Eccleston, the Formula One Tycoon to the party. Martin asked .....*Or have we slain one dragon only to have another take its place with a red rose in its mouth*? New Labour were not too pleased with that question and comment considering what support they invested into Martin's campaign. Martin went on to write a book in 2009 called *A Very British Revolution* which commented on the MP expense and allowance scandal.

Martin also commented on page 137 about *how falsehoods would be invented* and repeated and that he was accused of *being the puppet of... all people - Alistair Campbell*. I did however find it surprising that Martin felt it necessary to state on the next page of his book that the Labour Party *had a single liaison officer in the Tatton campaign whose job was to report back on progress.* Of *himself he also wrote that although he was an unlikely stooge the falsehoods would be recycled...* The fact was that rather than having just one single Labour Party Officer reporting back on progress as Martin said the Officer concerned was also working long hours organising the campaign, directing volunteers, including myself, preparing and facilitating leaflet origination and printing etc. Additionally as volunteer North West regional adviser I was requested by the Regional Director of the Labour Party to support Martin.

As well as Peter Bracken from Labour HQ there were many local Labour activists working with and supporting Martin throughout the campaign. This included the Labour Party prospective candidate who stood down to allow Martin to stand in the election. Martin went on to serve one full term of Parliament as he had promised and continues out of Parliament to be the media choice as the voice for honesty and integrity in politics. His opinions on political standards and independent MP scenarios are sought by the media on a regular basis. Over the years we have kept in touch from time to time about political standards and he provided words of support in a campaign I was fighting to save our local Children's A&E department.

He came up to the North West to do a charity fund-raiser I had arranged for the Tsunami appeal. We also raised funds for a local cause for a wonderful young lady challenged by cerebral palsy. Martin was both generous and kind to the family that night and gave a great speech. I stood on a chair and gave a speech also to all our guests that night, but that speech was overshadowed by the inspirational words spoken by the young ladies Mum. Martin was then Special Ambassador for the United Nations Children's fund at the time.

Martin has been active visiting countries like Darfur to try to raise the profile and seek support for those in need. To me that is what politics should be all about. Making a positive difference in the lives of others. He is not perfect as we all have our imperfections but he is the closest we have had to a model MP for others to benchmark.

5

THE DEMOCRACY TRUST

Martin Bell went on to serve as Tatton's MP until the next general election in 2001 when he stepped down. This decision was to meet the promise made to serve only one Parliamentary term if elected as MP. I'm sure he bitterly regretted his pledge made during the frenetic 1997 campaign. I believe he would have been happy to contest the seat to secure another term of office. In February 1999 I suggested that Martin should stand in the European elections as prospective Independent MEP. I had hoped he could have promoted higher standards of public service in Europe. However he decided not to and said it would be too much of a distraction *as the weight of the party machines would fall on him*. Martin had already experienced negative party machinery at work targeting him. This experience seemed in the form of a politically originated character assassination attempt.

Whilst a serving MP Martin had been very critical of many aspects of the political system and the New Labour approach. In particular his speech in Parliament in December 1997 asking *have we slain one dragon* (eg the previous discredited Tory Government) *only to have another take its place with a red rose in its mouth* (eg New Labour/new danger). The implication was that political sleaze etc was again at large in our country. Of course he was absolutely right in his description and as the years moved on New Labour presided over a decade of Parliamentary culture founded on spin, sleaze and a failure to deliver the purer than pure promises that Tony Blair made to the nation. Sometime after making his speech it was leaked to the media that Martin had incurred substantial legal costs during his Labour/Lib Dem supported election white knight campaign in 1997 and these costs had not been declared on his election expense returns.

An alleged breach of electoral law revealed an attempt no doubt to tarnish his whiter than white image. The source of the leak to the media is to date still unknown and senior political figures like Alistair Campbell have made it clear they had nothing to do with the leak. However it seems probable that the leak must have been sanctioned by a senior political insider. A high ranking person connected with the undeclared party funding/resources provided to support Martin's alleged independent campaign in 1997. Political insiders perhaps were increasingly concerned with Martin's challenges to the political establishment.

Martin and his Election Agent Kate Jones were blissfully unaware of any legal fees paid during the course of his 97 campaign by either the Labour or Lib-Dem parties. During the campaign they were aware however that legal opinion was made available by a legal expert who was then an adviser on electoral law etc to the Lib Dem party. Martin's political appeal to the voters was again to be tested in another part of the country. When it was known that Martin was giving up his Tatton seat he was asked to stand as Independent Candidate in Essex. This was to contest the sitting Conservative Candidate MP, Eric Pickles, in June 2001 at Brentwood and Ongar. Martin was effectively head-hunted by some local people and agreed to fight the seat as independent. At the time there were media reports of allegations by local people that the Constituency Conservative Association had been infiltrated by members of an evangelical church.

A somewhat different cause to fight than Tatton and a campaign without real merit considering all the other political issues and challenges at that time. I and others would not have advised Martin to pursue that seat. I was contacted by BBC Radio 4 and asked to take part in a interview going out on 5 live radio. I was interviewed about Martin Bell and Neil Hamilton followed with Neil's opinions in a separate interview. I visited the constituency during the Essex election and considered the campaign politics as puzzling, bizarre even, to myself and possibly others in the electorate. Some of the campaign literature strangely depicted Martin as a cartoon- like figure, which did not present his many qualities. It looked like the artwork was lifted from a Fred Flintstone cartoon. As it transpired Martin did not succeed with his new approach to politics in Essex.

The election results however gave Martin 32% of the vote against the sitting MP's 38% of the vote. Martin later went on to become Special Ambassador for the children's charity UNICEF with other celebrities to follow such as Robbie Williams and Jemima Khan. He is still consulted by the media a decade or more after his Tatton election victory regarding his views on standards in public life. What did result from the Tatton election however was focus and unrelenting interest on alleged sleaze in politics and public life, Martin Bell seemingly as the standard bearer for the cause.

The man in the white suit was still working to bring light and integrity to the grey world of party politics. With some original members of Martin's 1997 election campaign team with whom I kept in touch, I proposed forming a not for profit company to promote a small think tank, which we launched. We called it The Democracy Trust. We had our own web-site and a passion for changing politics and public service for the better. Fellow Directors Nick Grant and Sue Addison were, like me, passionate about high standards of public life and selfless service to the community by elected politicians and MPs in particular. Recent political history pre-2000 and ongoing revelations since reveal that many politicians indeed appear to be self-serving. We set up the Democracy Trust to promote higher standards in public life and to encourage politicians to forge a contract with the electorate to serve selflessly and solely for the common good. Our objective was published:

As stakeholders in democracy our aim is to achieve a democracy trusted by the people, accountable to the people and serving the will of the people. We believe that democratic processes are too important to be left in the care of career politicians. The erosion of democratic processes has been underway for some time now in many of the decision making structures in society. We intend, with your help, to halt this decline. With these aims in mind we will support and promote the standards outlined in the Seven principles of public life as specified by the UK parliamentary committee on standards in public life.

We also published on our web-site and leaflets the following introduction, which probably holds true a decade or more years on:

It is the belief of many that some elected politicians abuse the trust placed in them and seek to serve their own career and personal interests rather than working in the best interest of the people they represent. This is evident at all levels to varying degrees. Promises made by politicians to serve the many and not the few are not believed when the opinions of the democratic majority are ignored. For example majority viewpoints on funding the millennium dome, introducing GM foods, taxation policy on fuel etc appear all to be ignored by those in power. A perception exists that the electorate voted out an uncaring, arrogant, out of touch Government to replace it with another Government rapidly becoming arrogant and out of touch with the people.

The electorate is concerned also with erosion of accepted channels of accountability which affect established parliamentary/democratic processes. Cabinet decision making is sidelined, the upward rise of the Quango state continues, cronyism is rewarded by honours or by gifting positions of power to unelected appointees and party contributors. Of major concern also is the capitulation of free thinking by some, demonstrated by toady career politicians providing foundations for elective dictatorship. The suppression of individual thought and independent views, fixing of electoral mechanisms by electoral colleges, focus group and policy unit government are all symptoms of a decline in democratic processes.

The use of Special (political) Advisers by Ministers rather than seeking the views of fellow politicians or Civil Servants, attempts to control public opinion by inappropriate spinning and all contribute towards the democratic deficit. Prime Ministers Question Time reduced to a farce with time wasting (self praising) questions presented by career MPs. It is the belief of the electorate that politicians and those holding public office should, on appointment aim to achieve the highest possible standards. To this aim, to serve others for the greater good before personal gain or career interests should be the key objective. In supporting this aim the preservation and development of democratic processes and accountability supported by a framework of political standards should form the basis of a contract made with the office holder and those represented. This contract should be honoured at all times and form the cornerstone in a building block approach, with other political standards to produce a world class benchmark of democracy and political excellence in this new millennium.

Long serving MP Tony Benn was kind enough to allow us to use part of a speech he had made on our information leaflet, which he said:

The Cabinet has lost its importance. Parliament is taken for granted and the public is just manipulated by advertising techniques. Given all this, it is no wonder that people have such a poor opinion of the House of Commons and feels that no one listens to them and that all parties are the same. A revived, powerful Commons, which genuinely represents those who elected it, is the best way of restoring the balance..... We must not fail. Too much is at stake to allow ourselves as spectators condemned to watch our leaders govern us instead of becoming active in shaping our own future.

To maintain political balance we printed another quotation by Sir Winston Churchill on the Trust literature. Many years before Sir Winston had written:

The tendency of political parties to discourage individual thought and independent views may suggest one reason for the fact that Parliament has declined in public repute.... If our parliamentary institutions are to survive, it will not be because constituencies return tame, docile, subservient Members and try to stamp out every form of independent judgement.....

Past and recent highly respected politicians from opposing parties who had their fingers on the erratic pulse of British politics. Both expressing concerns about Parliamentary democracy, of which, issues are still unresolved as many of the elected few continue to fail the many of our society. The Democracy Trust also published a voter-focused MP code of conduct, which we believed was reasonable, achievable and met the needs of the electorate. The code and supporting letter was posted in 2001 to all 659 MPs in the House of Commons and to Members of the House of Lords. Our aim was to build on the Seven Principles of Public life as originally initiated by the previous Conservative Government and in theory adopted by the New Labour Government. We wished to extend the remit of principles to cover meaningful standards for an open democracy.

This included selfless service, an end to gravy train politics, enhanced freedom of information, equal opportunities, environmental protection, accountability to electorate etc. We believed the standard could be adopted for use by MEPs, Councillors, Quango Board members etc. In 2000 I wrote to Mark Seddon, Editor of the left wing Tribune publication asking him to consider publishing our proposed code of conduct for politicians. I didn't get a reply. Years later the code still stands the test of time considering the revelations about MPs paying members of their family etc from the public purse and claiming a variety of financial perks not afforded to the electorate.

I am sure that most reasonable people would wish to see the Parliamentary rules changed to bring the Right Honourable Members into the real world that all citizens are subject to in terms of financial control, accountability and value for money. The Democracy Trust Standard will hopefully continue to be promoted and perhaps one day this code or something similar will be used to bring honour back to the place of Honourable Members.

In 2001 only 56 out of the 659 MPs in the House Of Commons replied to the Democracy Trust letter and proposals with 26 MPs actually signing the code. It seemed that around 4% of all MPs shared our vision of a new Parliament, which could and should as the Mother of all Parliaments establish a benchmark of democratic standards for the rest of the world. Of the 26 MPs who endorsed the code one was Independent MP Martin Bell, another was the only Conservative MP to endorse, with 5 Liberal Democrats and 19 Labour MPs signing up to the standard. On the second of March 2001 one high profile female MP sent our literature back in apparent disgust and wrote on the form; *what is this rubbish*? She also wrote that ...*we already have the Neill Committee on Standards In Public Life - our own kangaroo court...politicians are answerable to their Constituents and their Associations who deal in rough justice for MPs who don't come up to scratch as you should be aware.* Well that was an interesting response we thought.

As it transpired that MP who had no time for our *rubbish* during her term of office, failed to declare some property interests. She was consequently suspended for a month for misleading the Commons' Standards and Privileges Committee. The committee alleged that she gave seriously misleading and inaccurate information to the committee. They also alleged that she breached the Westminster code of conduct for MPs by improperly contacting witnesses during the investigation. Her handwritten reply to us clearly appeared to reveal some degree of tension and frustration within her as demonstrated in particular with the words kangaroo court and rough justice being used.

A Member of the House wrote to us and said: Your trail dated 11th January has just reached me. It does not inspire confidence.... *For example tell me half a dozen names you have recruited, of whom I might have heard. Tell me where your money comes from, tell me what your intentions are, tell me if you have links to any of the political parties and if so which? Do not at this stage tell me anything else please.* Clearly he had not properly read our newsletter, nor our letter or visited our web-site.

Independent minded MP Dennis Skinner phoned and left a message on the Democracy Trust answerphone implying that our proposed code was not robust enough. He made various points including that of other MPs taking paid foreign trips and that MPs should not have any Directorships as they did not need extra income. He pointed out the fact that he had lived by his own code for public service for over thirty years. Clearly he was a man of strong public service principles and had not boarded the gravy train wagon as some MPs had. The Democracy Trust with minimal resources went on to provide limited support to some Independent candidates and groups around the country and contribute to various articles for local media, especially in Martin Bells' Tatton Constituency.

By a stroke of accident or design our trust was also listed on the web-site of the National Council of Voluntary Organisations as one of the leading think tanks in the UK. We felt quite flattered by that accolade to feature alongside the Hansard Society, The Royal Institute for International Affairs and other prestigious organisations. In November 2000 the Punch magazine had a very interesting article headed as *The Thoughts Of Chairman Mo*, which was written by Mohamed Al Fayed, Chairman of the Harrods Group. What he wrote then about politicians is still valid a decade on. He said:

Most people will not vote at the next general election because they are sickened by the corrupt way in which politicians have acted....The public have every right to feel disgust for the three major parties. But there is an alternative: they can vote for independent politicians, the majority of whom are clear thinking and honest people who are fed up with the way the country is going.... Britain wants open Government where politicians and civil servants are brought to account. And if that means replacing every MP in Parliament with people who stick to their own beliefs rather than political doctrines then so be it.

After reading his article again in 2004 I thought I should test whether he would be prepared to put his money where his mouth was. It should follow that if he believed independent MPs was a solution to our failing political system then he must be prepared to support that initiative. I contacted his office in October 2004 by phone and follow up letter. I reminded him about his article in 2000 and sought his support by saying: *My concern is that most independents lack the support infrastructure to mount a strong election campaign....Can you assist The Democracy Trust to help others achieve your vision of a better democracy?..... Do you know of any other influential people who can assist in our aims?* The office of Mohamed Al Fayed, Chairman of the Harrods Group did not reply to our enquiry, which was a shame because on this issue his heart seemed to be in the right place. Perhaps the letter, email and fax did not even get past his PA.

In my letter I did thank him for the financial support he gave to children's hospices which was not widely known. By email in 2010 I also contacted his office to ascertain whether his fighting talk could be translated into political activity. His assistant did broach the subject with him on this occasion but due to his retirement from Harrods he chose not to get involved. In March 2001 Martin Bell MP wrote to us and suggested *that recent events had made the maintenance of standards by MPs more important than ever.* He also suggested that *it may be a good time to seek an appropriate pledge* (against our MP code of conduct) *from the candidates seeking to succeed me in Tatton.* All the Tatton candidates gathered for a public meeting during the General Election campaign and I with some nervousness chaired the meeting, which was like a BBC Question Time event. The Labour, UKIP and three independent candidates agreed to endorse the code of conduct. The Liberal Democrat candidate and George Osborne, later to become Tatton Conservative MP and Chancellor of the Exchequer expressed support for the code but to the best of my knowledge did not actually sign up to it.

The Democracy Trust with limited resources and no monies assisted where it could and made contacts around the UK including a few meetings with Parliament's other Independent MP - Dr Richard Taylor and would-be political independents. I provided support to a local and newly formed independent political party - The Southport Party who did well to win three seats on the local council. Their main aim however was to obtain a breakaway autonomous town council from the sub-regional council and this was probably not achievable. They were principled people for public service but eventually lost their seats to the main parties. They also decided not to contest the general election, which I thought was tactically wrong and exist now as a party without electoral representation.

As part of my support role for the party during those early days I provided advice in respect of a campaign to oppose the closure of our town's children's Accident and Emergency Department. As a result of my community activist role I was to be targeted by party political nerds of the nasty kind, who demonstrated the dark side of human nature. One in particular, who later became a party approved prospective Lib Dem MP, suggested such enlightening advice to people on a web based forum as *go and abuse a donkey in the most imaginative manner* as well as defaming me. Some sad people in politics have a tendency to demonstrate foul rather than fair means when others attempt to develop alternative political and community benefit options.

Due to illness and other reasons in 2005 the Democracy Trust was put on the back burner until 2009 when the MP expense scandal was exposed by the Daily Telegraph. I like most people in the UK and abroad was appalled at the abuse of the MP expense and allowances system and this provided impetus to resurrecting the Democracy Trust.

I contacted various groups promoting higher standards and independents standing for Parliament and attended a meeting in London with Martin Bell and others at offices of the Independent Network. I invited a representative of Power2010, which was an innovative organisation established to promote democratic excellence. Prior to the meeting I met and sat with TV celebrity/ex jungle *I'm a celebrity - get me out of here* Esther Rantzen who was considering standing as an independent in the next general election.

I outlined some of the Democracy Trust principles and code of conduct for MPs. She made it quite clear then that she was reluctant to sign up to a code, which would prevent her as a MP working for the media during her time in Parliament. Esther did not actually commit herself by confirming she would definitely stand as an independent in the 2010 general election. She described her attitude at the time as *being on a cusp* whatever she meant by that. A month or so later I noticed her featured in a tabloid newspaper advertisement selling accident insurance claims to the readership. I wondered if she ever became an MP would she feel obliged to cease such income generating roles. During the meeting Martin Bell presented his own code of practice for MPs and left the meeting early. Although in general terms the Bell principles were ok there was no remedial action for MPs who breached his guidelines and he only covered a portion of the MPs actual and desired activities representing the electorate. The group without much real debate about the strengths and weaknesses accepted Martin's submission.

I then proposed they could consider the Trust code of which Martin Bell was the first MP to endorse in 2001. He backed up his original endorsement then with a letter of support for the initiative. The group managing the independent network were volunteers trying to make a living as well as trying to support people politics instead of party politics. At that time there were different groups operating in the country with similar or overlapping aims. I suggested that in the interest of reforming our democracy that the groups meet and produce an agreed strategy for those shared aims. Whether that independent coalition approach will transpire remains to be seen.

Due to lack of financial resources etcetera I produced my own very amateur website for the Democracy Trust until funds could be accessed to pay professional web designers. I contacted a few newspapers in an attempt to get the message out. But as with all lobby groups or any new initiative resources, money and influential people are needed to successfully take forward a vision and convert that into a reality. Yet again time will tell if democratic excellence will ever really be supported and pursued by those in power.

6

SAVING THE MINISTER

I was to be tested in court following a prolonged web forum tirade against me from a prospective MP (web chat room name *Tonio*) – who worked for my Lib Dem Constituency MP. The experience was somewhat balanced however by support from others who genuinely wanted to make a positive difference in people's lives. This political episode resulted in me taking legal action against Tonio contesting his web-based defamation. It also resulted in me having taxpayer funded pints of beer with the Deputy Leader of The House of Commons who had also came up against Tonio. The origins of the dispute and spin off events began when faceless and unaccountable bureaucrats in Whitehall and indeed the European Parliament made decisions that resulted in closing down our children's Accident & Emergency facility.

It caused outrage in our Constituency. It took me and others to the door of Number 10 Downing Street and resulted in words of support from Cherie Blair. It created political turmoil locally and strangely resulted in the saving of the seat of the Deputy Leader of the House. Sadly the tragic death of a baby some six years later on the way to the other hospital was one terrible event we all feared when we originally opposed the closure of children's A & E. A tragedy waiting to happen, which sadly did happen.

Allegedly the family were told they could not attend the nearest hospital during the emergency, which originally had catered for children's A&E. When the news was announced that our seaside town and constituency of around 60 thousand people with 5 million family visitors a year was to lose our children's

A & E department understandably most people were shocked. Reasons given for closing kids A&E included an independent enquiry recommending closure, the European Working Time Directive, shortage of specialist doctors and clinicians etc. The service was to be relocated about 8 miles away to a smaller town whose road links were poor and often jammed in the summer months. Opposition to the closure proposals from across the political spectrum was swift with local groups forming. I suggested in an article in the local media that a cross-party coalition was formed to fight the closure. I proposed that the campaign does not become a party political issue. Prophetic words perhaps as things turned out. I also suggested holding a public meeting for all parties concerned the following week and setting up a campaign coalition.

Out of the blue the local Lib Dem MP suddenly announced his own public meeting. I drew up campaign objectives, terms of reference, a code of conduct for members and information material with survey documentation etc. We made contact with local political representatives, the local Lib Dem MP and pressure groups and arranged our first public meeting. I eventually called the campaign CARES, Campaign Against Removal of Emergency and other Services. At that meeting and subsequent meetings it became clear that the local Lib Dems had their own strategy. For example the MP was speaking to media about having an NHS Walk In Centre, which to most campaigners was a glorified minor injury unit.

It was no substitute for an A & E department caring for children as well as adults. Some of the subsequent CARES meetings sadly ended up as slanging matches when a few senior local Lib Dem activists engaged in disruptive behaviour (some videoed) during the meetings. One would-be Councillor was holding mobile phone conversations during the meeting. Later I was to become a target in the form of defamation by Tonio. He was a long standing Lib Dem activist and paid researcher for the local MP.

CARES ran a very informative media campaign, met with the NHS Trust Chief Executive, held a massive protest march in the town followed by presenting the petition to the local Trust Board member. I politely spoke to the Board Member about our opposition to the planned closure, however I was somewhat perturbed as his trouser zip was open on view to the attending media cameras. Hopefully I didn't excite him too much.

The photograph of his failure to zip it still exists however with mischief-makers. I was later criticised by some political types for being too *aggressive* with the poor board member. I was attempting to defend our children's emergency services and believed I spoke from the heart. Aggression did not come into it. Afterwards we returned to the local park to meet the hundreds of people remaining who had been in the protest march. There was a microphone and platform in front of the waiting crowds but no real attempt by any member of the campaign team to address the crowd, to review things and talk about the way forward. I obtained the microphone and thanked the marchers for their support.

I was later criticised by some political types for making a so called political speech. It was in no way a political speech but I was criticised anyway by them. The criticism of my role continued in the form of defamatory postings against me on forums on a local web-site by the MPs taxpayer paid research assistant, who was funded to work for the benefit of local constituents but was strangely engaged in an unfounded campaign of untruths against me - who was working as a volunteer for the good of the local community. Even more surprising was the fact that his employer must or should have been aware of his actions and for some time took no positive action to curtail the inappropriate behaviour. His fixation on alluding to donkey abuse on his web forum postings was very strange to say the least and for him to be selected to stand as Lib Dem prospective candidate against a Government Minister in 2004/5 is even stranger. He had for some time been posting comments about me on the website forum attacking my honesty, my democratic values etc.

Some would describe the postings as a form of internet bullying or cyber staking. I never responded/retaliated nor posted anything on the forum chat room facility apart from news and press releases relevant to the hospital campaign etc. I therefore ignored his rantings for some time until people kept pointing out his defamatory postings about me. Apart from untruths posted about me, which were later confirmed as defamatory by Lawyers, he, under the name of Tonio and allegedly listed also as Serious Nerd, had over months posted strange statements in many postings openly accessible to the world wide web.

Some of his strange postings included: *abuse a donkey or two for me in an imaginative manner wont you?...which dumb helpless animals would you like us to abuse besides donkeys?... and what form of abuse would that take?... in Outer Mongolia where they tolerate donkey abusing fans of Nazi death dealing... I only post here to counter perpetual attempts at disinformation from the grandstanding splitters and their Nazi death machine acolyte - but then who knows in which hidden corner of Mongolia the cowardly Nazi death machine lurks.*

Well I suppose some would say the Liberal Democrats embrace a broad church membership and diversity of views. I decided that I would adopt a reasonable approach and talk to his employer, the local MP. I had met him briefly months before and outlined the situation but no remedial action was implemented. In November 2004 I arranged to see the MP again in a local pub. I politely put forward my concerns again about the smear campaign and my wish to seek an amicable resolution to the situation. I also mentioned that due to episodes of surgery I had that year etc I did not wish to have any other additional pressures on myself or my family. The MP informed me about his faith and how he was going to mass that weekend etc and that I should have faith in his representation of my interests. He promised he would get back to me. His promise was as mythical as the name of the pub that we had met in - The Arion.

Although being my MP I he failed to contact me after the meeting, nor did he proactively engage with me to resolve the issue in the following months. I eventually wrote to him by recorded delivery expressing my disappointment. As he had failed to help me as an individual and also as his constituent I decided to take the matter up with the Parliamentary Commissioner for Standards. I had presented my analysis of other aspects of his interpretation of serving his Constituents and I suggested that his judgement should be questioned when a key member of his staff posted strange web forum comments on donkey abuse etc.

I pointed out that it was beyond belief that this was allowed to go on unchecked by him as my MP. I finished my letter by saying that *...we are all human and make mistakes. Hopefully you will learn from this and perhaps do the right thing next time.* Over that period I had in the spirit of fairness supported the MP with an article in the local press to correct misinformation put out by the local Conservative Party, but that gesture from me was discarded apparently. I think he got the message from my letter and also my request for information under the data protection/freedom of information legislation. Much later on I, with all the other Constituents of that MP, was to receive a Lib Dem leaflet from his office saying that they are always trying to solve problems and *PS if you have a specific issue or personal problem you want addressed, or even raised in Parliament just email or phone me...*

Well when I needed help to resolve a ongoing problem from a key member of the MP's team it was not forthcoming. My complaint to the Sir Philip Mawer, Parliamentary Commissioner for Standards was that a member of the MPs staff had pursued a negative and defamatory campaign against me during times when he was paid to undertake parliamentary work on the MPs behalf and using facilities provided for parliamentary purposes. My detailed analysis of the time and day of week of the web forum postings showed many, many postings during normal office hours and this was a key part of my complaint. In April 2005 after reviewing the extensive folder of material I had provided Sir Philip contacted me with his decision. He said he could only consider the complaint in respect of the Code Of Conduct for Members approved by the House. He said that he could not comment on the substance of the postings and that Tonio had rejected my interpretation that his postings were defamatory.

The court was later to refute this assertion by Tonio. Sir Phillip's conclusion on the complaint made was based on information provided was that Tonio as a full-time employee working in the MP's Constituency office had *always worked flexitime*. Additionally whilst at work *he did not use taxpayer provided computers but used his own lap-top or an elderly PC belonging to the local Lib Dem party*. Sir Philip was told by the MP that after he met me he had spoken to Tonio who agreed not to engage in similar behaviour in the future and that Dr Pugh took reasonable steps to correct the conduct on Tonio's part... Sir Philip concluded that there was no breach of the Parliamentary code and no grounds to pursue the complaint. On 21st July 2006 on BBC 1 news Sir Phillip Mawer made a statement in which he said there was a need to strengthen public confidence in politicians. We are still waiting Sir Phillip.

At the Labour Party Conference in 2006 Chancellor, Gordon Brown MP, made a speech in which he said *we are servants of the people.* He also said his parents encouraged *all to live with a moral compass and that we must have a soul...* On 31st May 2009 Prime Minister Brown whilst interviewed on BBC's Andrew Marr Show stated that *we need a statutory code of conduct for MPs*. Democratic campaigner Baroness Dame Helena Kennedy QC suggested that *the citizens should play a lead role.* Whether these things will happen remains to be seen.

In my case the so-called Parliamentary codes and standards had failed the electorate. It had allowed a taxpayer funded MP's Assistant to mount a campaign of defamation on a member of the local community. The Commissioner for Standards accepted the *working flexitime* reason to explain away the office hours web postings. This acceptance of the MP's explanation without seeking time/diary analysis on postings was compounded by the strange explanation that constituency work was carried out *on a PC belonging to a political party* (data protection issues?) *and a laptop provided out of Tonio's own personal finances.*

He also decided that alleged defamation be discounted although extensive evidence had also been presented with legal opinion. He also accepted without question that the MP had resolved the issues. The issues had clearly not been resolved and he had never followed up by making contact with the constituent he should have been representing. A test of Parliamentary standards for me with the guardian of those so-called standards in my opinion failing to implement the world class excellence that the Mother of All Parliaments deserved.

Tactically I had a Plan B in place in the form of me pursuing direct legal action. I had sought legal advice from a City Law firm and had also researched the legal issues myself. Prior to that I had gained experience in around twelve successful cases of litigation representing myself and others through the Small Claims Courts and Employment Tribunals. I had always trusted people like those I had loaned money to and had expected service providers to deliver what my family had been charged for and also expected committed employees not to be unfairly dismissed. I always try to be ethical and fair in my life but if anybody abuses trust or fails to deliver what is paid for then I seek justice and fairness. A serious litigant perhaps rather than a serial litigant.

I had presented my summary and bulging file of alleged defamation by Tonio. The Lawyers considered it and agreed with me that the content via the web forum Tonio was defamatory. They wrote to Tonio with a copy to the web-site owners to point out the legal situation and potential action to seek resolution via the courts. One day in response to the Solicitor's letters a rather formidable man knocked on my door and introduced himself as representing the web/forum company. I invited him in and he proceeded to tell me that *he was known by the local police etc.* That could have been either a positive or a negative bit of information, I thought. It was scary as I had never met him before, he was in my house and I thought shit - what have I got myself into? As it turned out his web company removed the offending defamatory web postings and we eventually enjoyed a friendly relationship going forward.

My solicitors had told me that we had a strong case to take Tonio to the High Court but it would cost tens of thousands and he may not have the assets to pay up against a successful judgement. I couldn't possibly afford the up-front costs and didn't want the stress and hassle that came with it. I also knew that Tonio had a young daughter and had no wish to see her indirectly suffer. I decided to take him to a small claims court to recover my legal fees and expenses incurred. My Lawyers never suggested this as an alternative option, which disappointed me so I consequently paid them off.

I believed it was quite rare to deal with defamation in a small claims court but I thought I would give it a go anyway. Tonio responded to the court summons by denying defamation and dismissing my claim. We had one court appearance with me representing myself and I met up with him outside and expressed my wish to settle the issue amicably. He did not respond and failed to attend the next court hearing. I presented my case and the Judge found in my favour. On the 24th November 2005 - the court made an order against Tonio:

It is ordered that the Defendants application to set aside judgement be dismissed. That the Claimant do have summary judgement pursuant to 5.8 Defamation Act 1996. The Defendant to pay Claimant damages ... in the total sum of £1143.00 by 30th November 2005.

The irony of the judgement was that Tonio had offered advice in some of his many postings about what constituted defamation. He went on to send me a cheque for the full amount and it went into my account. But some weeks later just after Christmas my bank wrote to me to say: Our clearing department has made us aware that this cheque has been lost whilst being processed. What it does mean is that we cannot currently confirm that if the bank that it is drawn on, are happy to pay the cheque for their customer. After an expensive Christmas I thought this was a disaster and wondered if someone was playing games. My vision was of a self-destructive cheque in cyber space and a big hole in our finances. The monies remained in our account fortunately and I breathed a sigh of relief. Well at least Tonio paid the financial price for his campaign against his boss's constituent, but he still kept his job. Years on he was still getting paid by the taxpayer to protect the interests of people like me. Tonio was selected in 2004/5 to be the prospective parliamentary candidate to fight the Oldham and Saddleworth Constituency on behalf of the Lib Dems. I don't know how their selection process worked however.

I'am sure they must have done their homework to the best of their ability to get their best and brightest candidate in place. The seat with the Tonio candidate in place was a winnable set for the Lib Dems especially with the aftermath of the Iraq war resented in many sections of the community. The sitting Labour MP, Phil Woolas, Minister and Deputy Leader of the House, had a fight on his hands and I offered to help him to prevent Tonio becoming a highly paid advocate of the people and species donkey. Phil Woolas MP invited me down to the House of Commons and took me for a few subsidised pints to the Strangers Bar with his assistant.

I outlined the background of my experiences with Tonio and said I would be happy to provide him with all the web forum details etc including the donkey abuse material etc. Phil told me that Tonio had made unfounded allegations against him including what was alleged in the local media in Oldham as *astonishing slurs*. Phil was seeking legal advice and asked for copies from my case file against Tonio to support his case. I provided the originals but it took my repeated calls to have them returned to me from his office. I mentioned the campaign I was involved in to prevent the closure of our children's A & E department and Phil seemed supportive. However I did stress that if I helped him I would not expect anything in return.

He did suggest that perhaps his legal advisers would be prepared to look at my defamation case at the same time as his own. That never happened. Phil used my information in his election campaign against Tonio and retained his seat at the General Election. How much of my input was a factor in his success is an unknown factor. We did lose the battle to keep kids A & E in our town and sympathy was all I got from the politicians. Much later I was to see Phil Woolas being interviewed by a friend, Tony Wilson, a North West TV broadcaster.

The subject matter for some reason was public toilets and the Minister appeared very concerned about the state and availability of public loos. Some could perhaps say that the sewage Tonio directed at him was a precursor to greater things. Phil was in 2009 to suffer the criticism of the national media for comments he made regarding immigration policy etc in his capacity as Immigration Minister. He was also to suffer the wrath and good sense proposals made by Actress/Campaigner Joanna Lumley during a televised skirmish on the plight of the Ghurkhas in the UK.

Tonio must have been greatly amused in seeing his opponent getting negative media coverage.

I was amazed in 2010 to see Phil Woolas stripped of his seat in the Commons because of allegations against him that he broke electoral law with untrue allegations in his general election campaign material that year. Politics is a strange profession. As a promoter and supporter of principled independent politics and high standards of political service I decided to practice what I preached and stand as Independent Candidate on a Save Our Children's A & E ticket. This was for the General Election 2005 and I linked in with a national support network for Independent candidates with a small political party registered with three candidates to stand across the UK. I was one of the chosen three and the party was registered with the name *Your Party*. Although I realised that without substantial financial and human resources there was a very remote chance of winning the seat I thought I would go for it anyway.

During the campaign my wife and I were invited to Reg Key's campaign office in Tony Blair's constituency where Martin Bell was providing support and advice. Reg was the father of a British soldier killed in Iraq under tragic and allegedly preventable circumstances. He and other families of British servicemen killed in Iraq were mounting a campaign against the Labour Government seeking the truth over issues in Iraq and seeking to influence Government policy. My wife Karen spoke with other grieving families that day and was in tears listening to their stories. We had our photo taken with Reg Keys and Martin Bell but it didn't turn out for some reason.

Tony Blair went on to retain his parliamentary seat at that election but he and Cherie must have been very moved by the passionate speech Reg Keys made that night with Tony and Cherie Blair standing alongside of them. I later emailed Cherie about that election moment but she didn't respond on that point. In my Your Party campaign I had excellent support from a graphic/web designer and others who produced first class election materials such as posters and media material. Money was found to produce a four page (front and back) election address etc in the town's tabloid newspaper with photographs, policies etc. *Bill can win* was the main headline with photographs of myself, my wife and I on each page. Quite embarrassing really for both of us but PR deemed necessary for election purposes.

Ex MP Martin Bell was glad to provide a written endorsement for the election address kindly describing me as a man of great integrity. A very rich supporter based near Swindon loaned a large box van for advertising purposes and delivering garden election signs etc. The van had adhesive election posters on all its sides and was definitely a first in terms of a new highly visible approach to electioneering in our town. I parked it on the main town road and in other key locations around the town. I also introduced a web-based survey into my election web-site for local constituents to be consulted on. I wasn't too well at the time following surgery and was limited in terms of what I could physically do. Knocking on the doors of thousands of households was out of the question. Family, friends and supporters helped where they could however with leafleting and poster sites etc.

I produced a 100 point constituent policy document covering local, national and international issues supported by a web based survey on those issues. I discovered that a public meeting had been arranged at a local church to meet the candidates. I didn't get an invite so I invited myself along. When I had previously spoken to a church official he said he did not have my phone number and couldn't find it. Strange I thought considering I had been in the local phone book for 23 years or so. I sat on the candidate panel faced the audience and gave a speech, which wasn't my best due to recent nasal surgery affecting my voice projection. On the night of the election I took along a small party of supporters and awaited the results. I received about 580 votes, which I was thankful for and the sitting Lib Dem MP was voted back in, which meant of course that Tonio secured his job of serving the electorate and local indigenous donkey community.

Each candidate made a small speech, with the Lib Dem MP quick to attack the Conservatives from the stage. I can't remember him thanking the vote counters or the local Council Officers for their election work. I and the other candidates did thank them. I shook hands with all the other candidates but the MP, John Pugh, looked at me like I was donkey dirt and ignored my outstretched hand. I quickly forgave apparent his rudeness towards me.

Although I failed to win the seat I had at least had a go I thought and the experience was worthwhile. Perhaps that experience could help other would-be political candidates in the future who wish to inject independent, representational values into the House of Parliament. Again I thought of gurus words of advice given to me years before that life is not about success or failure as they are both experiences to learn from. The down-side of the campaign was the abusive phone calls in the early hours of the morning when most ordinary people were sleeping. Abuse targeted against innocent people in my family from faceless people who had in my mind lost their soul along the way. I recorded the abuse and met with the local police but the perpetrator is yet to be identified. Natural justice will perhaps manifest one day.

7

No 10 JOURNAL - WAGING PEACE ON IRAQ

It was after leaving The Labour Party that I commenced my email exchange and occasional encounters with Cherie Blair. The journey moved on to five-year virtual dialogue, shared smiles, photographs, some words, jokes, warm handshakes and linked arms with the first lady, Cherie Blair. Perhaps someday she will regret giving me her book inscribed with the words *To Bill my email friend.* Her responses to me over those years originated from both the small rooms the Blair's used above No 11 Downing Street and the contrasting opulence and expanse of country home Chequers. Email dialogue with Cherie was most probably monitored by the security services with the same security spooks perhaps doing their homework on me. Maybe some scrutiny into my background and a risk assessment into my contact. Perhaps looking at my motives with the Prime Minister's wife. On some occasions I wished the unseen spooks *a good day* or a *happy Christmas* on phone calls made to friends. A silly thing to do perhaps, but if some calls had been monitored I at least provided some humour to the bored operative.

In the flesh Cherie certainly appears more attractive than the media portrays and she has nice eyes and instant rapport with people she meets. Cherie certainly made an impression and gave hope to a lovely teenage girl with a challenging disability I had arranged for her to meet. She told the girl she could be *anything she wanted in this world* or words to that effect and gave her and her family great inspiration. That same inspiration for others I was seeking from Cherie to champion a cause was sadly not offered to me during the campaign to prevent her hospice closure a few years later. She was to respond promptly to me by private email over the years and experience my constructive criticism as well as support. The last time we met at No 10 Downing Street she walked towards me, saying *hello Bill* in a posh legal accent unlike her Liverpudlian origins and linked my arm. She virtually dragged me into position for a photograph as I noticed the sparkle in her brown eyes and became aware of her expensive perfume.

It made me think of another time and another place when the wife of another Prime Minister was so close to me - a mere commoner. That was Norma Major, many years before who during a visit with Prime Minister John Major accidentally brushed into me and my folded arms in the crowded National Exhibition Centre, Birmingham. Her right wing firm breasts rubbed along my arms when she squeezed past me. I didn't get too excited about that fleeting accidental encounter with the PM's wife though. Some years later I was to engage in conversation with ex MP Edwina Currie who was allegedly close to Prime Minister Major.

In the future I cannot see myself as making any contact, accidental or otherwise, with the wife of a third British Prime Minister on my life journey. They say things happen in threes - so who knows what fate brings? Apart from our Liverpool roots, perhaps the only thing Cherie and I had in common is that we both experienced some poor times in our early years, and sang pop song(s) thousands of miles away on the over side of the world to those poor students in China. Apart from the singing efforts of Cherie one memorable occasion comes to mind. Cherie performing like Royalty with a shiny spade digging a hole for a small tree, whilst us commoners watched from a respectful distance. Her Security Protection Officer scanning the surrounding woods of that hospice for signs of danger lurking amongst the red squirrel and wood pigeon inhabitants.

The photograph of her digging a hole as a potential source of much mischief-making if the Private Eye magazine ever got their hands on it. Perhaps our generation, our mutual scouse profile laced with a working class rebellious streak was the foundation for mutual interest in politics, pop music and aspirations to change the world for the better. I first met Cherie Booth and her famous other half, Cherie Blair during a visit the Blairs were making to North Wales with the Welsh politician Ron Davies, pioneer of Welsh devolution. He was later to leave the Labour Cabinet in 1998.

Ron came across to me as a nice guy with a strong Welsh handshake and a mischievous wink. Cherie was travelling across Wales with her husband, now Prime Minister and Mr Davies were hosts for a business lunch. This was in a hotel near Chester for a few select business people and supporters.

The Labour Party and Ron must have been short of bums on seats to invite me or perhaps they were desperate for my dazzling contribution. I wasn't too impressed with Tony's after lunch speech but he did say hello, briefly chat and I was soon talking with Cherie. I asked her did she know a relative who went to the same school as her. Like Cherie the relative was a Barrister and of a similar age. Whether she remembered her or not she didn't seem that interested. My daughter Lucy knowing I was to meet the PM and his wife had written a nice card and enclosed a photograph of herself for Cherie to pass on to her daughter Kathryn. She was around Lucy's age then, about ten years old. Lucy and I were to check the post every morning for weeks afterwards for a reply to the letter, which Cherie had taken. Her wait was in vain and the mail from No 10 didn't arrive.

Sadly the photograph given to Cherie was a treasured one of Lucy with no copy and Cherie's staff probably binned it somewhere en-route back to No 10. It was a shame that one brief letter, even from a No 10 secretary to Lucy wasn't sent.

That would have given Lucy a thrill. After that contact with Cherie we were to meet again during Blair's ten year reign in office. The start point for my emails was in December 2002 when it became clear she was having a really bad time with the Foster allegations and Carole Caplin connection, which dominated the media at the time.

I was at a later stage to suggest more than once that the Blairs set up a Blair/Booth Foundation for worldwide charitable aims. I would tease Cherie over a few years on how her book was going before it was a news item. She emailed to say our paths may cross during a visit to Liverpool but she didn't take up my offer to do a Beatles song together in a Liverpool karaoke bar. I first wrote to Cherie's email address at her law firm - Matrix Law.

Sent: 11 December 2002 16:09
To: cherie - - - -
Subject: Good luck and best wishes/Democracy Trust

Dear Mrs Booth
Just a note to say that a lot of people on Merseyside and beyond are supporting you during this difficult time. The following letter has gone to various newspapers. Whether it is printed or not is another matter. Best wishes and for speaking the truth, from the heart Tuesday evening.

Dear Editor
Re: Cherie Blair

The Democracy Trust, which has its origins in the 1997 Martin Bell v Neil Hamilton General Election campaign in Tatton has been a strong supporter of independent politics, democratic standards and enhanced integrity in public life. In particular The Trust supports the seven principles of public life that this Government has signed up to but yet to fully deliver: Honesty, Integrity, Selflessness, Leadership, Objectivity, Openness and Accountability. The media have indeed raised many pertinent questions about the role of civil servants and the 'spin machinery', which have been brought into play on behalf of Mrs Blair, a private citizen and not an elected politician. It would appear that up to Tuesday's statement by Mrs Blair the 'spin' had spiralled badly out of control and fragmented her full account of the issues.

Mrs Blair appears not to have done anything illegal or improper in conducting family business transactions within a hectic life-style and dealing with friends and others on face value as we are all 'guilty' of. Seeking character references of acquaintances in private life never happens and in this unique high profile situation this has resulted in an unfortunate chain of events. Most people would certainly not have described Mr Foster as a financial advisor in the role he did play. Mrs Blair can only be guilty of trusting people, using and trusting the No 10 machinery until things go badly wrong.

Hindsight is a wonderful thing, but we are all human and so is the Prime Minister's wife. What most people are not aware of is that Mrs Blair is a Christian activist as demonstrated by her frequent and unpublicised visits locally, on Merseyside and beyond to support hospices and other good causes. This selfless part of her busy life-style is not reported in the media. The media should be bringing balance and perspective to the personal issues arising and now allow her and her family to move on and focus on matters important to most people. The role of civil servants and the No 10 machinery is a separate issue to address by learning the mistakes made in the past and more recently.

My letter was actually printed in the Daily Mail newspaper and Cherie wrote back with her thanks and appreciation a day later from Downing Street after getting my email. She did not use her Matrix law email address this time, but used the Downing Street email address:

From: cnewcourt@no10.x.gsi.gov.uk (Cherie Booth)
Subject RE: Good luck and best wishes/Democracy Trust
12/12/2002 17:33:02 GMT Standard Time

It was pleasing to get some words of appreciation from Cherie Booth. The next correspondence with Cherie was just before the invasion of Iraq. It was my attempt as an equal citizen of this world to influence another equal but more powerful person, the Prime Minister, to fly out to Iraq to broker a peaceful solution. I sincerely believed at that time, as many did that based on speeches from Blair and others in Government, that Saddam had weapons of mass destruction. It was beyond doubt that Saddam had authorised the massacre of countless thousands of innocent people by gassing peaceful villages and other inhumane acts. However I, as others believed that the Prime Minister on behalf of UK citizens should have attempted to broker a peaceful

134

solution before any bombs were dropped. Even if President Bush and the American hawks opposed such an initiative it was worth a try to avoid war. It is on record that Blair's Government and even John Major's Government had previously engaged in dialogue with those described as terrorists to broker peace. Dialogue behind the scenes with one-time pariahs who had pursued a political agenda whilst perpetrating use of terror bombings, bullets and violence. On 19th February 2003 I decided to email Cherie with a proposal aimed at avoiding the allies waging war on Iraq with leading to massive loss of life for innocent civilians caught up in the warfare.

Subject: Support/President Bush etc - Dear Ms Booth Private and Confidential

I did write to you recently and had a letter of support for you printed in the Daily Mail re the recent problems concerning Mr Foster etc. You/Your office replied to me using your email address. I had lunch with you and your husband in N Wales some years ago re Ron Davies dinner and spoke to you about Barbara Ryan (employment law Barrister) who knew you from school days. (When we met I passed you a letter/photo from my daughter Lucy to your daughter - of which Lucy did not get a reply). I have been down to No 10 and No 11 and helped on a regional and national basis to get the PM/Party into office. Since then I have moved on formed the Democracy Trust for different reasons. To get to the point I have always believed that any political differences I have with Government had for some years been overshadowed by my longstanding belief that your husband had a mission to fulfil in facing up to threats of a global nature. Tony showed his courage/moral policies in the Kosovo conflict and at the risk of

135

sounding cranky (as a Christian) I believe destiny has put him into this situation and he still has a major role to play in addressing global problems. Like all of us he is human, has doubts and probably under massive pressure in finding a balance to avoid loss of life now and in the future. My proposal is that he takes the initiative/turns the situation around by flying out to Iraq and speaking directly with the dictator in search of a solution acceptable to Britain and America.

If there is a small chance that this provides a solution then he should grasp the opportunity. If Saddam fails to respond then nobody can say that Tony did not, at some risk make an attempt at the 11th hour. This offer by Tony would be welcomed and respected by all and contribute to the resolution of the serious issues raised. It is ok for me to suggest this but I would be happy to put my life on hold, leave my family and go with him or his representatives. Please give this proposal some thought. I am not a crank but a Christian and democrat (who today put my signature alongside that of your father and 100 others to seek regional government in the North West).

Last night on TV the US President called your husband a courageous man. Perhaps a visit to Iraq with or without the blessing of our allies will take that courage forward again.

I wish your family well during this difficult time.

Bill

I got a swift thank you reply the next day from Cherie and she said she would pass on my proposal. Of course Tony Blair did not fly out to persuade Saddam to step down and the rest is history. The ongoing turmoil continues but allegedly more peaceful indicators are slowly emerging. My proposal was clearly unacceptable in light of the United States determination to go to war and to export democracy down the barrel of a gun in exchange for barrels of another sort. However a few years later I was to discover that pre-invasion Sir Richard Branson of Virgin business empire had a plane on standby ready to fly to Iraq. His idea was for Nelson Mandela and he to fly to Iraq to broker a deal to avoid the war. Koffi Annan, Secretary General of the United Nations supported the initiative. Unfortunately the bombing and invasion by the Allies started before they could fly out.

We can only guess how history could have been changed and perhaps hundreds of thousands of lives saved if my proposal or the Branson/Mandela plan had been successfully implemented. I still passionately believe that we are all equal in this world. Our actions, our input no matter how small can create a positive ripple effect across the world, ideally for the good of all. If I was Blair I would have flown out in an effort to encourage Saddam to stand down and prevent the invasion. He had nothing to lose and everything to gain by attempting peaceful diplomacy and lives are still lost every day in the aftermath of that invasion.

History shows that politics is too important an agent for positive change to be left solely in the hands of politicians. My experience of politicians in general supports my belief that even the most educated politician may lack commonsense, relevant life acquired skills and have lost sight of what they are in public service for. Their position of power often elevates them to a position on a pedestal where people have to raise their eyes to look up to them. However my attempt to influence world stage decision makers is I believe a right we all have. We are all created equal and no one can take that away from us. It was reported in the media that Sir Richard Branson was establishing a forum of eminent people called The Elders initiative to promote world peace and reconciliation. I wrote to Sir Richard and asked him whether the initiative had any opportunity for an ordinary person like myself to be involved or is it just for the great and the good, rich and powerful of this world? I didn't get a reply and contacted his office but it seems my enquiry must have gone into the recycling bin. Still I suppose we can only try. In March 2003 I watched Tony Blair giving an inspirational speech in Parliament about facing up to the dictator Saddam.

At the time and based on the evidence presented I believed his policy was correct. I did find it appropriate in what the Prime Minister was saying in facing the evil and threat that Saddam posed with weapons of mass destruction. As a Christian, what again also came to mind was an extract from speeches made by both Blair and Deputy Prime Minister, John Prescott over the years: *I am my brother's keeper*. I believed, as I still do that we are all brothers and sisters in this world and that it was and is our duty to intervene to protect others. I believed that if no other options exist, apart from do nothing, that well thought out intervention is justified. Perhaps like good samaritans it is our collective duty not to ignore the suffering of others.

I thought of the systematic killing of Kurds, Marsh Arabs and ethnic minorities in Iraq, the murders in the Kuwait invasion by Saddam and his evil supporters and I totally supported Blair in toppling Saddam. I genuinely but perhaps naively as it turned out, believed it would bring rapid peace and freedom, save countless lives and bring stability to Iraq. As the decision to invade was fait accompli and probably made in meetings in the USA with President Bush a year or so before, I felt I had to respect his decision to go to war, as clearly he had decided to ignore the peaceful approach. I believed Blair's policy would eradicate the alleged weapons of mass destruction, which of course never existed. I was utterly wrong in my perception of the post-war outcome considering the hell that was unleashed on many innocents in Iraq.

But who knows just how many more innocents would have ended up in the killing fields of Iraq and beyond if Saddam was still in power for another decade or more. Perhaps he would eventually have unleashed even greater forces of killing power if he had not met the hangman. It was interesting to see that some years later Tony Blair flew to Libya to embrace dictator Gadhafi using a diplomatic strategy, which was not in evidence in his approach, pre-Iraq war, in dealing with Saddam. I also believed then that Tony Blair had a destiny to fulfil in resolving global conflict and suffering and he had made a good start in working to secure peace in the Balkan countries and other places and undoubtedly saved countless lives.

I also could see the strain in his face on TV and had wondered about the constant stress he and his family were under because of his world role. It was later reported four years later in a TV documentary of the Blair years that the PM was not eating well and feeling very down over that period. The Blairs were a family as we were with human frailties and emotions but I and others expected some super-human outcomes with the power Blair had. After all his party preached their party anthem - *things can only get better*. Like all of us we are perhaps victims or authors of our own destiny.

8

No 10 JOURNAL - DISILLUSIONED DISCIPLE

I knew Cherie Blair/Booth, like many people, myself included and based on my own personal experiences had a great interest in spiritual matters so I passed on to her details of what I believed was a thought provoking website - thewayoftheheart.com. This was about people's life purpose or life mission on earth and I believed it had sensible content, which would have practical meaning for all who viewed the site. My niece Jo had discovered the website whilst working near Woodstock in America. After watching a memorable speech by Prime Minister Blair in Parliament I sent Cherie an email, which included my belief at that time in Tony Blair's destiny in world affairs, a destiny and life-mission partly achieved but with much more that could have been done.

Myself like many ordinary people and decision makers believed the security intelligence and Prime Minister Blair's submissions that Saddam Hussain had weapons of mass destruction and was a mass murderer to be dealt with by international intervention. What most people and I didn't know at the time was the overwhelming evidence to go to war including the twenty minutes time-scale for Iraq to unleash WMD was totally misleading. A claim never to be substantiated by supporting evidence and follow up enquiries. It was a case of either the Government had not been competent in obtaining accurate intelligence information or, as many alleged *sexing up* and misrepresenting the evidence.

The email I sent to Cherie 18th March 2003 was based on my total belief at that time in the evidence the Prime Minister had presented to Parliament and the nation. Subsequent revelations alleged in 2009 by high-ranking British officials indicated that the Blair Government had decided in agreement with the USA that regime change was the reason for waging war.

Subject: Support etc
Dear Ms Booth

I am sure that after watching your husband today in Parliament that your resolve has been strengthened. He inspired me. As a Christian he is taking the right path and as a consequence countless families will in future live free from fear, the loss of loved ones and the dark forces of evil from Saddam and others. I passionately believe that in this crisis your husband is fulfilling a destiny, with you at his side with faith in your heart and a key role to play. Today Saddam made reference to 'God's will, which illustrates his concept of good and evil. I believe that it is God's will that your husband takes a stand against this evil force and in the process weathers the formidable storms unleashed which could sap the strength and will of men of lesser conviction than he. You have concerns of the immense pressure placed on your husband and the burdens he carries un-refreshed by sleep. He is without question doing the right thing in facing evil, you are doing the right thing in your support, even after wrestling with your thoughts. Unwritten history will endorse the rightness of the course taken, the courage shown. You and your family will in time move forward to a new life phase of peace and normality and engage in other aspects of your life mission. I believe the legacy you both wish to leave is to make a positive difference in people's lives along the way. I share those views although the strategy and resources are indeed different. As a man who married a 'good catholic convent girl' and with a family

142

including a daughter of similar age to yours and normal family problems I cannot imagine the day to day pressures you are facing during this time. It is in the spirit of appreciation what you must be experiencing and support that I write to you. I am sure that you are v busy so I wont expect a reply. May God go with you and give you strength during the difficult days and nights ahead. For your interest a web-site with interesting reading is http://thewayoftheheart.com (it has nothing to do with romance by the way)

Best wishes
Bill

I again got a quick reply from Cherie and she said she knew the road I lived on and was confident that the Prime Minister was doing the right thing. On my side I had got it totally wrong in believing the political misrepresentation of the facts and I was supporting military action, which could possibly have been avoided. Cherie was of course totally supportive of her husband on this issue, presumably after reviewing all the facts that she was party to. On leaving office Mr Blair is engaged in part-time peace- making on the world stage, especially in the Middle East. Let's hope he achieves more in waging peace instead of waging war. A searching public enquiry may in the course of time indeed confirm that the Iraq war could have been prevented by other options available. My next email to Cherie was a request for a high profile guest speaker at a charity dinner near Liverpool. As a Liverpool girl, Liverpudlians (known as *scousers*) are generally known for their sense of humour.

For a joke I decided to submit my guest speaker request as though it was intended for Carole Caplin, her companion/aide much targeted by the media during the

Foster Financial Adviser situation. I don't think Cherie saw the joke, or if she did she ignored it completely as one would in her position - just like royalty perhaps. She did kindly agree however to attend an event for charity. I also proposed by email then 8th June 2003 that she and Mr Blair establish a Blair/Booth Foundation for charitable aims around the world. As Cherie spent much of her childhood living, playing and schooling some ten minutes or so from where I spent my youth I introduced some local interest to grab her attention. I was genuinely impressed with media reports on the vast range of charitable causes she supported.

Subject: The Blair (Booth ?) Foundation/Jospice

Dear Ms Booth

Private and confidential

When I had my letter published in the Daily Mail 13/12/02 in support of you when the media was not so pleasant I mentioned the support you gave to hospices etc. Today in the M.O.S. magazine I am both amazed and delighted at the enormous range of support activities you are indeed involved in. The article was enlightening, inspiring and showed through you what life should be about - making a difference in people's lives. I wish more people would follow your path and focus on selfless rather than selfish pursuits. I am really delighted that what you are doing from your heart is recognised and is appreciated by those you meet and from today, more further afield. For many years now I have provided some pro-bono support etc to many charities and small businesses, social enterprises, including hospices victim support, The Prince's Trust, Blind Aid Society etc. I am currently assisting a small charity based in South Road, Waterloo who provide furniture to families in need and working with the Jospice Association based in Thornton and other 'clients'. I have recently formalised this support into The Business Trust (Co Ltd by guarantee) who provide support to beneficiaries with free or highly subsidised services. Although The Business Trust has had no public monies or support offered from any Govt agency or external funder on Merseyside we have been listed as runners up in the Liverpool Post/Echo Regional Business Awards community support awards - June 19th. United Utilities and MBNA credit card co are the other two runners up.

To the point, I would like to ask you if you could facilitate/suggest a high profile guest speaker for a fund-raising event I would like to arrange in Formby Hall Golf Club in the Autumn. I would, subject to discussion, like to offer two thirds of the funds raised to the Jospice based in Thornton and the remaining funds raised for the Business Trust so that we could provide more resources to help other charities etc. Ideally the guest speaker should be attractive, good fashion sense, with a nice smile, 40 something with a high profile ticket selling potential. She should have an independent mind, a warm heart, a strong spiritual side, great integrity, good humour and principles. If Carole Caplin couldn't make it, would you ?. oops - scouse joke.

Perhaps when you move from Downing St you may consider a Blair/Booth Foundation to carry on the good work you are doing on a national/international level. The work I am doing with others on Merseyside links to your life mission perhaps with some synergy, albeit with far little resources. If I can be of any assistance to your overall aims in any way in this non-political work then I would be pleased to assist. Did you ever look at

145

thewayoftheheart.com web-site by the way ?-life mission

I am really pleased for you with today's article. The Prime Minister was right on Iraq and I hope people will move on and appreciate what he has done to make the world a better place with our allies.

Best wishes again

Bill

She replied the same day and said she had done some stuff for the hospice before and suggested that 2004 would be a better time in her diary. A hospice fund-raising lunch was eventually organised in January 2005 with Cherie as Guest Speaker. My next email was to tell Cherie I was visiting Downing Street for the third time, but this time not actually getting over the door-step of No 10 or 11. I helped form a cross-party/community supported campaign group opposing the loss of children's accident and emergency, maternity and other services at our local hospital. The group's representatives and myself as a disillusioned Blair disciple were to deliver a 20,000 signatory petition to the Prime Minister. By email on 14th February 2004 I presented a nine point list of Government failures to Cherie and I also suggested that Mr Blair would lose that opportunity to be considered a great Prime Minister if he carried on his path.

I also touched on a failure by the Labour Party to honour an auction prize I won, which was actually confirmed in writing in September 1996 regarding Drinks and Lunch with Tony Blair and John Prescott. Cherie didn't react to my gentle hint but what actually happened was a sum of money was pledged/paid to

Labour Party funds by myself at a Coronation Street set fund-raising dinner. The great and the good of the Labour hierarchy were there including Blair and Prescott. I was daft enough to bid for the privilege of having lunch and drinks with them as the promised prize down in Westminster. On reflection I suppose it could be considered by some as a solicited cash for access scenario.

Albeit under public scrutiny with over two hundred people or more movers and shakers in attendance at the dinner. My passion then was getting Blair and Prescott and the party into power and was happy to contribute what I could for the cause. I was however very pissed off never to receive my intimate lunch and drinks with them both. I wonder is it too late to sue for breach of contract? I also suggested that Tony Blair could eventually leave Downing Street as a disillusioned and bitter man if things continue as they do. Perhaps he is disillusioned because most people probably believed he never made a great Prime Minister nor left a lasting legacy to be cherished.

Subject: No 10 visit/strong spirit etc
Dear Ms Booth

Private and confidential

Re: Visit to No 10.

Last year I set up a group in Southport called CARES to try to restore our lost A&E dept for babies/children and many other patient service losses to a community, which also has 7 million (family) visitors a year to the resort my child and other children at risk. After spending many years raising tens of thousands of pounds for New Labour and making many personal sacrifices of time, personal monies and dedication to contributing to LP electoral victories I find myself with an appointment with five colleagues to knock on the door of No 10 next Thurs 19th Feb - 2.00pm with a petition of some 20000 signatories opposing the New Labour health model in our community. 3000 Southport families joined our protest march and this issue will not go away. Feedback of 'near misses' from paramedics are emerging of kids lives being gambled with this flawed policy.

If you are at home and happen to look out the window on Thursday I am the tall dark/greying scouser in a suit with a weak heart and a strong spirit.

Weak heart/strong spirit: In confidence:

On a personal note I hope the Prime Minister is in good health and taking your advice. I am a similar age to Mr Blair. On Fri 13th 1992 without warning/medical history I had a major heart attack/cardiac arrest whilst working away from home in the Lake District. Subsequently I had a further three related and two unrelated life threatening encounters. What it did for me was to attempt to cram in as much as I could of what really matters in life, as my health would allow. Priorities do change as you will know and I am sure that the PM's aim is to complete his mission to make a positive difference in the lives of our nation before he leaves office. Some years ago I was invited to give a presentation to LP GSec Tom Sawyer on how to harness the volunteer base of the LP membership. This followed a personal case study I produced; then as a new member for David Evans LP Regional Sec. I then would have walked over hot coals for Mr Blair to get him into power. Things have changed and if I am typical of a disillusioned and saddened New Labour 'disciple' then the PM will be leaving Downing Street somewhat disillusioned and possibly a bitter man if things continue as they do. As a 'disciple' of the PM he took me to the top of the mountain and I didn't like what I saw on the other side and I walked back alone to the valley from whence I came. My experiences in politics lead me to believe that Labour will lose the next election if the current path taken continues.

With respect I believe that the PM may leave office considered as a good PM but will if things don't change will miss that wonderful opportunity he had to be considered as a great PM. He showed immense courage in world affairs in Kosovo, etc. However history may only recall the 'control freak' administration, Hutton, WMD etc and issues described below. Going from a totally dedicated supporter/contributor to campaigner against many LP policies I would urge him to re-evaluate his life mission and return to that what I believed he was hoping to achieve in power. My experiences have influenced me to speak from the heart, weak as it is as life is too short. We are a family as you are, you have immense power we do not. I respect the position you both hold but we are all equals - hence my comments today. What you consider me to be is your decision and if I am constructively to the point then so be it. I believe in the 'Ripple Effect' of how individuals can sometimes affect wide ranging situations - as per that web-site I suggested to you some time ago. You have a good heart and kind spirit and much more to achieve.

The PM has got to get back on track for peace of mind, fulfil his destiny and not let the millions of people down that invested so much hope in him as Leader. You are rightfully loyal and may object to my analysis, but I can assure you in the real world away from big business and glamour the third way has gone pear shaped. Thank you for listening and my hope for good health and peace of mind to you all. I will promise not to send unsolicited emails to you again. I have said what I would have said to the PM if the documented offer of lunch with him at Parliament would have been honoured at Parliament by the LP. (following Coronation St dinner some time ago).

Thank you again for the work you do for charities, which largely goes unreported. Your support to hospices in particular is much appreciated here on Merseyside and beyond.

Best wishes

Bill

PS

New Labour Failures to address:

- From grass roots party democracy to House of Lords and European integration democratic processes have been gradually eroding since 1997. Parliamentary accountability has been whittled away by many different methods. This needs to be recovered and confidence rebuilt.
- Business confidence and especially support for small businesses has worsened under this Government. 3 million people who work in small businesses are turned off by this Government's policies.
- This Government promised to reduce the Quango state - it has grown immensely instead.
- Although as a Christian I support a multi-ethnic society the economic migrant issue and shambles that it

is will be a major factor in bringing down this Government.

- Policy on health is not working and groups are forming all over the UK to fight service losses. Growth of admin staff is greater than clinicians under this Government.

- Policy on GM crop growing in the UK is totally against wishes of the majority and displays arrogance and 'in bed' with big business/USA influence.

- 'Tough on crime and the causes of crime' has failed and the Government has lost credibility as a result.

- What has happened to the 'Stakeholder' society aspiration. It is never mentioned now and people are listened to but then ignored. eg closing down kids A & E and kids ward against the wishes of 98% of the local community (survey result 2003).

- Hospices not sufficiently funded by the state. (Frank Dobson as H Sec once told me that 'they do very well at fundraising anyway' eg dont need Govt money).

She thanked me for the email, said she was in court so would miss the petition. It was good of her to wish us luck with the petition against kids A & E closure and she did say she would pass on my comments to Tony. However many of the issues listed like Quangos are still unresolved years later. In December 2009 nearly five years later Prime Minister Brown's Government announced radical plans to reduce the number of Quangos. Too little too late yet again and fire-fighting reactions rather than strategic planning that the public deserve. It also highlighted the Ministerial failure to manage the public administration and finances in a timely manner. Regarding the point I made about the migrant shambles the Home Office on behalf of the Government conducted a public survey published in December 2007, which found that 77% of

151

people wanted a strict limit on immigrant numbers. The survey found that 68% of those questioned said there were too many immigrants in the UK and that they were dissatisfied with Government action on immigration and asylum.

Comments she made about my twin in a private section of that email indicated that she had misread my email. I had of course gone straight for the jugular in respect of my criticism and wonder did she actually pass on to Tony my analysis. My point that Parliamentary accountability was being whittled away and the fact that Mr Blair would lose the opportunity to be considered as a great Prime Minister was perhaps borne out by events since that email in 2004, especially by the revelations about Iraq pre-war so called planning and aftermath. The scandal of MP expense/allowances was undoubtedly alive and well during the Blair years in office.

9

No 10 JOURNAL - STRONG SPIRIT, WEAK HEART

Cherie Blair had been a long-time supporter of a Hospice in Crosby near Liverpool named the Jospice charity. The main hospice site was in Cherie's home-town, Crosby, Liverpool with a smaller site based in Ormskirk, Lancashire about 8 miles away. Jospice also supported some overseas hospices in South America and other countries. With Cherie's old school-friend Pat Murphy, who was the hospice charity fund-raising manager we organised a hospice fund-raising business lunch at Liverpool's largest riverside hotel in January 2005. I got a brief mention in the speeches and Cherie as guest speaker gave a strong speech about the work of the hospice and supporters. She also made everyone in the audience aware of some additional monies the Government had put into the hospice network that year, an announcement I thought perhaps somewhat political for a charitable event.

The monies were only a drop in the ocean anyway and miniscule to what the government was to find for banking support some years later and the billions of misspent public expenditure over the thirteen years of government. Government funding for hospice running costs in 2005 was only around 6% of total running costs for children's hospices and around 33% for adult hospices. On a purely economic level UK hospices save £millions of taxpayer money, reduce so called bed blocking and are a perfect community based model for public money investment. To further develop hospice care at patient's homes as piloted successfully by Merseyside based Queenscourt Hospice is yet another much needed service that governments need to invest in. After my wife and I cared for my terminally ill mother-in-law at home for nearly a year the support given by Queenscourt was a godsend and for some nights we could sleep soundly knowing that carers with special skills and love to give were on duty in our home.

At the fund-raising event Cherie came over to speak to guests on our table and was very nice to me, my family and guests including a teenage girl living with a challenging disability. Cherie spent much appreciated time with her and gave her inspiration. Many photos were taken and Cherie was kind enough to remark on how attractive my wife and daughter were, which they are I believe. A member of the hospice staff alleged that Cherie's dinner plate was swimming with gravy and they were not too impressed with the hotel service. Afterwards people queued to have photographs taken with Cherie and she asked me to provide her with a copy photograph, which I later did. Some days after the event the media were having a go at Cherie again about alleged fees for overseas speaking engagements.

I wrote to her 30th January 2005 to thank her for the charity fund-raiser and to offer support because of the press criticism. I also mentioned her reported singing episode in China and wrote to her about her reported interest in psychic type events. Being an identical twin with experience of many unexplained psychic type situations and myself researching such matters I touched upon that subject. I was some years later to document my experiences around my life challenges, following my heart attack and growing involvement in unexplained but fascinating psychic experiences etc which did indeed have a basis in a strong spirit and weak heart.

Subject: Jospice and other matters
Dear Ms Booth

Confidential:

From the guy at the jospice dinner with, in your words the very attractive wife and daughter : (Re your song in China. I actually went to China a year or so before you and coincidently was asked by Chinese College students (City of Nanning) to sing a Beatles song. I sang Yesterday and then followed up with Unchained melody. Beat you to it as international singer. Perhaps we can make a CD together for charity. (Know any good guitarists?)

Jospice:

If I may build on all the thanks already given for you making the Jospice Event on Friday such a successful occasion for all who attended. In particular the lovely xxxxx, who was the young girl whom you found time to chat to was over the moon with your kind words and attention. Her mum passed in a card and note to me yesterday which said:

The event gave xxxxx a real confidence boost as when we tell her she can be anything she wants to be it doesn't carry the clout quite as much as when she is told the same thing by Cherie Blair. Thank you so much for making such a positive difference to her life. xxxxx has had so much to live with in her 15 years of life and her family are having to pay for Chiropractor treatment un-funded by the NHS. You have a heart of gold and this I believe is part of your destiny to work to make this world a better place. The key to complete peace of mind is where you are going and the good you do which comes to you so naturally.

Media:

I see the press are having a go at you again. I hope you don't mind but I have written to most of the press today (copy available below - will they print it though?) to point out the negativity, lack of balance and potential inaccuracy of their reporting. xxxxx mum, I and others are appalled at their unfounded campaign against you. Some say the media hype goes with the job but the lack of balance is unfair to say the least.

Dear Editor

Starts:
Once again we read in newspapers of an ongoing campaign to present the worst possible picture of the Prime Minister's wife for her alleged fee earning as a keynote speaker at foreign events. Whatever truth lies below the media speculation Ms Booth should be admired as a tireless and dedicated supporter of charities and good causes in this country. She gives her time freely to those countless good causes. In the process she is of course not fee earning in her role as QC. I was at such an event on Friday afternoon in Liverpool where Ms Booth was guest speaker for a charity with hospices around the globe. Ms Booth spent a lot of time at our table with a young girl facing challenges with her Cerebral Palsy condition. I had a note from the girl's mum today saying:
The event gave our daughter a real confidence boost as when we tell her she can be anything she wants to be it doesn't carry the same clout as being told the same thing by Cherie Blair'. My point is that the media should present a balanced report on the issues and recognise that Ms Booth is a sincere, kind and generous person whose heart is in the right place. She

certainly made a memorable and positive difference to the life of one lovely teenager on Friday. Perhaps the press should list the great number of good cause engagements Cherie is involved in over the year to balance the negative press reports. For the record I am not a supporter of Mr Blair's Government and for many reasons would be delighted if he sought a life outside of politics.

Ends

Strictly Private and Confidential Stuff:

Is it true that you have an interest in psychic/spiritual matters? I for many reasons (as a Christian) have studied/experienced these areas. Am a member of The London College Of Psychic Studies. I have had eight life threatening experiences and survived, lost an older brother who drowned before I as a Twin was born. I went on to save four different people from drowning in separate situations and have had numerous other amazing experiences I wont relate here. If you do have an interest in this subject then please let me know. I don't share this private element of my life widely for various reasons. If you need reference points as to my good character or otherwise then L.Party Ann McCartney/Ian McCartney know me, as does Andy Rowe working with the First Minister in Scotland. I am also assisting Phil Woolas MP (Dep Leader of the Commons) currently to get him re-elected - although I am not a party member or supporter of some of this Government's policies. And of course Pat Murphy knows me well - but not of above confidential stuff. Thank you once again and best wishes. As they say in Liverpool you are a star.

Bill

Cherie responded quickly with a thank you to me for the kind words and confirmed that she was delighted that the young girl got such a boost from the meeting. In respect of my enquiry on her psychic interest she suggested that she always had an open mind to some of the mysterious aspects of life. Following the successful general election for Labour in May 2005 I sent Cherie a note of congratulation and touched on some UK and international issues. At the election count in Tony Blair's constituency the Blair's unease standing next to opposing Independent candidate Reg Keys was very noticeable. The words of Mr Keys were a poignant reminder to the PM of the effect his decision-making made on ordinary people's lives with lives lost. Reg Keys' son had been killed serving in Iraq in tragic circumstances and Reg fought a long and dignified campaign about the futility of that war and the human cost. Some weeks before on 30th April 2005 I had sent an email of support to Reg Keys' campaign press officer. Amongst other things it said that:

The Iraq war demonstrated the dangers from within our democracy and political system as well as the dangers faced globally. Until evidence was produced to show there was no real threat of weapons of mass destruction I, like many believed Mr Blair's claims. The WMD claim, combined with my views on Saddam's massacres of his own people led me to support the removal of Saddam in the interest of world peace. I like many believed the threat was real and imminent. .... Mr Blair flew out to Libya to meet President Gadhafi to facilitate Libya's policy change and secure agreement from Gadhafi to destroy his weapons of mass destruction (nuclear/biological and chemical etc) and to secure the ending of Gadhafi's support to terrorists, eg Lockerbie plane bombing. Mr

Blair was quoted as saying: when we have to take action, we take action. Where we can by diplomacy and negotiation bring people to a more sensible strategy for the future, let us also do that. Events proved that Mr Blair's decision not to use diplomacy in Iraq was wrong and the British people misinformed pre the invasion. Sadly the result has been for Mr Keys a tragic and unnecessary loss of his son's life.

Tom died and tens of thousands of innocent families also experienced death, bereavement, maiming, homelessness, fear and despair. As a one time 'disciple' of Mr Blair I walked the New Labour 'third way' - to the top of a dark mountain. I saw black clouds over our democracy and a perilous abyss on the other side. It was then that I parted company with New Labour in search of a path promoting true democratic accountability, integrity, selflessness and above all ethical leadership in our society. I fully support Reg Keys in his efforts to gain justice, accountability, and a political system to replace the Blair administration, which fails us all. The people of this country deserve more than a battered democracy in disrepute. We are all human, we all make mistakes - even Prime Ministers. However the sign of a great and genuine leader is that mistakes are admitted, the common good comes before political ambition and arrogance plays no part in service of the people for the people.

It was revealing that some years later when Tony Blair was first appeared at the enquiry into the Iraq war it was reported that he offered no words of comfort to the families of service people present in the room. Some broke down and cried when he said he had no regrets about removing Saddam, but he did not respond to the feelings of grief with words of sorrow about the loved ones killed. On 7th May 2005 I sent the following email:

Subject: Congratulations and other things

Dear Ms Booth
Congratulations on the election result. However God's greatest gift to you it seems is your family around you - this comes across strongly. The Prime Minister is blessed to have such a loyal and loving wife and lovely family beside him through life's journey. I have 5 children and a daughter (Lucy) of Kathryn's age. You met Lucy/my wife also with .... and her mum at the Crowne Plaza 28th Jan 05. Politics to me is the means of making a positive difference in people's lives and the work goes on. You may recall I took a 20000 petition down to No 10 re the closure of our kids A&E here in Southport. I stood in the GE on the hospital ticket in Southport but sadly failed to rid our town of the LDem MP. In Feb 2003 I suggested to you by email that (pre the Iraq invasion) the PM fly to Iraq with or without the blessing of our allies to broker a peaceful settlement. I suggested that if Saddam fails to respond then nobody can say that Tony did not at some risk make an attempt at the 11th hour. We cannot re-write history but as the Prime Minister said outside No 10 - 'I have listened to the people...........I believe he spoke from the heart. Looking in your eyes and those of the Prime Minister during the Reg Key's speech it was plain to see that as parents you were both deeply moved but constrained by what was politically correct at that time. I went up to see Reg in Sedgefield with my wife Karen and Karen ended up in tears when she spoke to another bereaved father whose son was also killed with Mr Keys' son in Iraq. I am sure that you can can understand the pain

Reg is feeling and his motives as a good and noble father of his son.

Yet again at the risk of being presumptuous may I suggest that the PM considers some positive action now to move forward and make this world a better place - for starters by:

1) Flying out to Darfur/Sudan plus brokering strong UN action to bring a swift end to the genocide, rape and pillage of 1.5 million of our brothers and sisters in our community here on earth. There is no oil there people will say, his mission will be noble and shame the superpowers. Suffering abounds as we enjoy our lives, homes and families in safety.

2) That the PM announce a (windfall) ring fenced tax of say one fifth of a penny on products or services that directly affect people's health. The tax be used to fund all hospices in the UK.

I know you are v busy so thanks for your time. I do believe that you have much more to achieve in your life for the good of all and that is part of your destiny. I believe you feel that yourself and have done for most of your life. I wish you well in that mission. You may recall that I told you that I have faced death many times in my life, was blessed with the gift of saving four people from death during my lifetime and have things to achieve before I move on. If I can also be a small but positive cog in the life and destiny of people with the power to do greater good then I can but try. We are all equal. With Pat Murphy we are hoping to arrange a large 320 person Jospice fund-raising dinner at Anfield early 2006. Perhaps we can say hello there - if not before. (I am free for a cup of tea for meeting such a good heart as yourself anytime). A heart to heart with the PM would be good but who am I - just a poor lad from Bootle with a weak heart, a strong spirit and no time to waste.

Best wishes to you and your family. God bless

PS at the Crowne Plaza dinner you asked for a photograph (I think) as attached.

Bill

Cherie replied with thanks for the note and photograph. She agreed that more should be done for hospices. We are still waiting. As for the tragedy of Darfur she suggested that a UN Security Council agreement was the only way forward. Of course that option was not stopping Prime Minister Blair from personally intervening and visiting Darfur/the Sudan etc to promote a cessation to the violence. Her response was so swift being within two hours of my email that I quickly sent another email of appreciation and some references to places myself (and Cherie) may have visited in our youth. It was only later that I thought - oops I hope she didn't associate my reference to binge drinking with the problem her son had when he was found allegedly the worst for drink in central London.

Subject: Re: Congratulations and other things

Hi

Gosh - your quick response is most kind and appreciated. Must make a dash to the cash machine to loan Lucy money for her 'girly' night out in Liverpool - with warnings from me about the dangers of 'binge drinking'. Hope she doesn't take after me as during my days at the Beachcomber/Mardi Gras etc L/pool also -

St Lukes Church hall dances in your home town Crosby..

Thanks v much and good luck on those two issues.
Best wishes
Bill

I got a quick thanks from her in response. Cherie was getting a hard time in the media following the successful general election win by the Labour Government. I decided to send her a note of support yet again but also included more policy ideas in the form of an electorate focused code of conduct for MPs to sign up to. I was hoping she would pass it on to her loved one - the Prime Minister - to implement. I also suggested paying MPs a higher salary and banning other paid jobs, preventing nepotism etc. Four years later the MP expense scandal was to shock the nation and my proposal was perhaps somewhat prophetic. On a mischievous note I also asked her 12th June 2005 whether it was Gordon Brown or Tony Blair driving the initiative to reduce the debt of developing countries. She quickly put me straight on that one - Tony Blair was the driver.

Subject: The Words of Winston Churchill

Dear Miss Booth

Winston Churchill once said:

We make a living by what we get, but we make a life by what we give.

I'm sure you have 'broad shoulders' to a point in facing all the political/media rubbish about you and don't need support. However this recent barrage against you is unjustified and grossly unfair when balanced against what you could be earning in your professional life when you do choose to give your time freely to so many charities etc. The time and energy you put into good causes is ignored. The same politicians who join the Desperate House Knives in Parliament to stick the knife in, have collectively failed to address the real abuse of roles of public service by MPs who engage in/ignore nepotism such as 'employed' spouses etc, public funded (undeserved) perks and acquired consultancies and directorships resulting in substantial private income for many MPs who should be working only for their constituents.

That is the hypocrisy of the negative campaign against you. You are a private individual and have served your country well since moving to No 11 eight years ago and your balance sheet of giving or taking is very high on the credit side. In Churchill's words you are a true giver from what I know of you - but that is not coming across in the media. I'm sure when you leave office eventually the Blair/Booth Foundation will have a positive impact on many lives. (Perhaps the Prime Minister should review Standards in the House and work towards a system whereby all MPs are paid a new rate and consultancies and acquired directorships/nepotism etc in office are forbidden) please see attached. This time the 4 newspapers I sent a support letter to (3rd June) did not print it. Best wishes in trying to make this world a better place.

PS the Govt initiative to reduce the third world debt is brilliant. Is it a Govt or Brown or Blair initiative as it comes across as a Brown initiative?

I know you are v busy and do not expect a reply. Bill

She replied again with a thank you saying my words gave her great consolation. She confirmed that the Prime Minister was very much the driving force behind the third world debt initiative. After the public transport terrorist bombing atrocities in central London in July 2005 I sent Cherie a note of support when all good people stood shocked but united against the killing and maiming of innocent commuters. Some time later via a contact, myself and a colleague were to visit the 7/7 charity in London caring for the victims and their families of tube and bus bombings to offer support.

Subject: United against evil

Dear Miss Booth

Just a note to say the Prime Minister is the best possible leader the world has to address this evil affecting our world. His speech today was what the country/our world needs and the approach taken is the only way forward. All people of love and good faith are totally behind him in the terror challenges facing us. Two and half years ago I wrote to you by email and said: 'It is my long standing belief that your husband had a mission to fulfil in facing up to threats of a global nature. I believe destiny has put him in this situation and he still has a major role to play in addressing global problems'. May God give you all the strength and safe passage on your mission to overcome terror and evil. (Although 'safe' in Southport/Liverpool ? I have booked to visit London and will do so as often as I can - they will never win nor extinguish our spirit in this battle against the forces of evil).
Best wishes

Bill

I got a thank you and I then gave Cherie a break from my unwanted opinions and suggestions for some months until ongoing frustration with politicians reactivated the passion in me for a better world. Unfolding political events, an out of touch Government and the subtle but effective eroding of civil liberties and free speech was underway. Alleged democratic management control as demonstrated by the banning of protesters outside Parliament, the eviction of the aged Labour Party member/heckler from conference were some examples of what really concerned me and many others. Declining standards in public life was acceptable to those in power and although more of a sinner than a saint I passionately believed that elected politicians and public servants should have integrity and high ethics.

Tony Blair promised on the steps of No 10 Downing Street be purer than pure and therefore an example to all when he took office. Cherie was a human rights advocate and allegedly more to the political left than Tony - she would I was certain share my concerns about freedom and democratic rights in our country. However my remark to Cherie that Tony's reign would be remembered more for a stable economy, as it was then in 2005, probably touched a nerve.

To most people the credit for the successful economy then would go to the Chancellor of the Exchequer - Gordon Brown. Although many believe that the foundation for the stable economy was laid down by the previous Conservative Government when the New Labour Government took on the Conservative spending formula in 1997. I did introduce in what I believed was a tactful way a comment on the life-style of the Blairs who lived a Christian Catholic approach to life whilst also enjoying a life-style like privileged royalty. Peter Mandleson said that Tony Blair would always take a bible with him and read it every night. Alistair Campbell said Tony would always have to find a church on a Sunday to attend. Labour Prime Minister Harold Wilson led a modest off duty life- style with holidays in the UK. As a Christian I found it disappointing that whilst the Blairs were on holiday, courtesy allegedly of politician/millionaire Bellesconi in Italy that the Darfur tragedy was unfolding and thousands of Christians/non-Christians were losing their homes, getting raped and killed. As Prime Minister I would have flown home from holiday or on to the Sudan as I felt it would have been the thing to do in an effort to halt the killing. On 5th March 2006 I wrote and reminded her of my previous opinions supported by my personal analysis of New Labour's government record to-date:

Subject: Three Years On
Dear Ms Booth

Three years ago, Pre-Iraq Invasion, I wrote to you to say that:

I believe that it is God's will that your husband takes a stand against this evil force (eg: Saddam) and in the process weathers the formidable storms unleashed which would sap the strength and will of men of lesser conviction than he...... I passionately believe that in this crisis your husband is fulfilling a destiny, with you at his side, with faith in your heart and a key role to play.......I believe that the legacy you both wish to leave is to make a positive difference in people's lives along the way. The Prime Minister was right on intervention in Bosnia and Kosovo. Based on the evidence at the time I supported the Iraq invasion and the removal of an evil dictator. In hindsight however, as a Christian perhaps George Bush or another world statesman as I suggested pre-Iraq invasion could have flown to Iraq to negotiate a peaceful solution. The formidable storms unleashed, immense loss of life, terrorism and potential civil war surpasses anybody's worst forecast of the aftermath. Who knows however, in terms of what other greater evils Saddam would have unleashed on the world, the Kurds, the marsh Arabs etc if still in power. As a one time passionate supporter of new labour, I put my heart, soul and resources into getting new labour into power. I try to see the good in all but am struggling with progress as I now see it. I can see the good intentions that new labour policies are trying to achieve but am disappointed in the legacy the Blair years will be leaving behind, policies apparently based on a Christian foundation. I have survived death many times in my life, faced many challenges and experienced many extraordinary events. What I do believe passionately as a Christian, albeit a sinner rather than a saint, is that we live our short lives here to make a positive difference in the lives of others. Politics is the vehicle for delivering those changes. You have met my daughter and my wife - my concern is that I would like to leave them with a better society when I move on.

My fear for their future is that democracy has been eroding away with our hard won freedoms haemorrhaging under the new labour project. 'Tough' decisions are now being taken with a macho delivery to explain away further state control and interference with our lives. More control on our freedoms, a green light for the use of torture by third parties, law making by the un-elected, the weakening of the judiciary, rewards for the party contributors of wealth and a blind eye to declining standards in public life - now much worse than under Tory rule. Arbitrary arrest for peaceful democratic protest by lone women, old men at conference.

Near to your heart perhaps - insufficient public monies into Hospices and the care of the dying yet vast sums found to fund useless 'initiatives', computer systems, ID cards etc, etc. Perhaps this Government is badly advised/out of touch. Perhaps arrogant behind the walls of power. Sounds familiar I'm afraid. Maybe I have got it wrong - I believed a Christian Democratic philosophy was based on embracing a simple but fruitful sort of life as Jesus and the disciples did and many others since - like the founder of The Jospice perhaps. Putting the needs of others first, leading by example with high standards, careful, not wasteful, giving rather than taking etc. In these caring measures and standards the new labour project has sadly failed and quite honestly if I and others, the teachers, the clinicians etc were asked to list the main achievements since 1997 it would probably be the economy that stands out on the credit side with probably a longer list of negatives and failings on the debit side. On the positive side there is still a way forward with the time left to turn things around like Christians often do. To admit mistakes, put others first and dogma and spin last. Politics should be making a positive difference in people's lives with freedom, democracy and care at the heart of what is delivered.

To lead by example, doing the right thing and using all political resources in the Christian way showing that power, wealth and associated influence are used for the common good. Life is too short to waste time and suffer regret later.Politicians are I know 'damned if they do and damned if they don't' and cannot please all the people. However as a 'customer' of new labour and ex member of the team, me and

169

many, many more will be putting our custom elsewhere based on a failure to deliver, even when the resources were available and the philosophy/mission was good - widely communicated but never met. It is for example a sad and disappointing situation whereas I, who would have walked over hot coals to get Mr Blair into Downing Street, that if I would ever wish to hand out leaflets outside Downing Street criticising this Government for the points raised and more - I would be locked up and gain a criminal record perhaps for doing so without police permission. Thanks for listening. There is still time to make maximum impact before leaving office but the clock is ticking. Who am I some may ask to be critical and tell the 12th most powerful woman on earth and one of the most powerful men on this earth how to run this country. I am just a lowly Bootle lad, son of a docker, who when a boy enjoyed jam butties and lemonade bottles full of tap water at picnics on Seaforth beach. Of course under God we are all equal, we all have a life mission.....We can only try.

Best wishes

Bill

She replied expressing her sorrow about my disillusionment and pointing out that Tony would always be a man of principle. She said she believed the Labour successes were more than just the economy and that last Friday she was in Newcastle opening up three children's centres, which would never had happened if it were not for Labour's policies. She suggested I should not lose heart. Well Cherie's loyalty was firmly rooted and I got the message loud and clear even if he was described by Cherie as a man of *principal* rather than a man of *principle*. In 2009 Prime Minister Brown got into the national news for his spelling mistakes to members of the public, so perhaps it was a No 10 thing on some outgoing correspondence. On the economy I suppose Cherie was lulled into a false sense of security as we all were that the prudent Chancellor was managing the economy well. What later came to light were the monumental errors of judgement and fiscal management by the New Labour dream team of experts. Notably the decision by Gordon Brown in 1999 to sell off 400 tonnes of UK gold reserves at under $300 an ounce raising £2.3 billion. In 2010 the prudent Chancellor would have netted around £10 billion if he would have waited for the price of gold to move up in price. Additionally it is worth noting that Nobel winner Joseph Stiglitz estimated that Blair and Brown's decision to engage in the Iraq/ Afghanistan conflict was to cost the UK in excess of 11 billion dollars

10

No 10 JOURNAL - P.UP IN A BREWERY

In May 2006 I was becoming more and more frustrated with the incompetence of the ruling political class and I wrote to her again. The message I sent implied politely that the Government couldn't organise a piss up in a brewery. Amongst other issues I mentioned were my hopes for the Blair/Booth Foundation concept again. I provided her with a standards framework for MPs to sign up to. Worth a try I thought. I commented on her working on her next book, which was just a hunch of mine and would help her to maintain the life-style she was used to on leaving Downing Street. I probably pissed her off a bit, especially when I politely reminded her of the things can only get better pledge and official anthem of New Labour. The email I sent on 1st May 2006 also included one example of some of the psychic events in my life:

Subject: Nine years on
Dear Ms Booth

A few years ago by email I touched on psychic events in my life, as a twin etc, etc, which can be validated by many - (including a senior person in a Govt Ministry). We all have a role to play in life and my Christian faith drives me hence again this email. Some six or so years ago I said to a few people including Andy Rowe of the L. Party (who went on to become special adviser to the first minister of Scotland) that: The Prime Minister would come unstuck with a blonde lady contributing to his loss of authority and that John Prescott would suffer some health challenge along the way. Clearly I got the names mixed up in my prophecy. I am not of course looking for a comment on private matters but thought you may be interested when you write your next book. I have offered advice pre Iraq Invasion, advice on standards in public life, hospice funding etc, etc. (Only last week I was in London to visit/advise pro bono a children's hospice who only get about £28 k per annum public monies towards £1.5 Million costs per annum.) Cost of keeping Foreign prisoners in our jails = £380 million......) The bottom line is that this Govt has lost its soul along the way and looking at recent events the expression couldn't organise a drinks party in a brewery comes into mind if you know what I mean.

A few years ago I sent you the document below, which only 26 (mostly Labour MPs endorsed in 2001). It still holds true now. I intend to resend to all MPs. Why genuine/credible/ethical politicians (including the PM who was sent a copy) could not endorse it I will never know. In 2001 I also wrote the following for a think tank, which again still holds true today: In return for being elected and vested with the authority to represent them the electorate is entitled to expect the highest level of service and professionalism from their elected representatives. High standards of unselfish service will be a vital element in restoring the electorate's distrust of politicians and those in public office who often appear to be serving personal interests rather than the public interest. I admit to hoping I could through you effect change for the better with your influence. I have failed of course. You are indeed loyal and I respect that but the quality of Government advice/strategy/outcomes leaves a lot to be desired. Life is too short, the need is great and much more could be done to make a positive difference to people's lives. Political standards have declined under labour, freedoms are being chipped away. The list of negatives dwarfs the positives. Locally - as well as closing down Southport's kids A&E 'Business Consultants' are talking about closing down adults A&E -- a resort with 6 million visitors a year. Patient choice, patient involvement mantra etc spouted by Ministers? A credible health service policy? Alder Hey kids hospital to lose millions of funding...(I have been around a bit by the way - Adviser to NHS, Plcs, not for profit sector, politicians etc). Perhaps more will be achieved outside of public life with the Blair/Booth Foundation in years to come and that charities/hospice patients, families in Darfur etc will feel the benefits. Time will tell. Best of luck - things can only get better as the song goes.

Regards

Bill

Political Standards (PS2K2) General Election Candidate: Member of Parliament Standard:

As a holder or prospective holder of public office I promise to support, promote and uphold at all times the following standards:

1. To act solely in the public interest as specified within the seven principles of public life* in both spirit and compliance: Selflessness, Integrity, Objectivity, Accountability, Openness, Honesty and Leadership.
(*The Nolan/Neill Committee recommendations - House of Commons on standards in Public Life).
2. To comply with in terms of accuracy, compliance, timeliness and without mis-interpretation all current standards and codes of conduct including register of

interests and statutory requirements of the appropriate public office.

3. To preserve existing democratic processes and promote development of enhanced democratic processes in all aspects of public life and politics in particular.

4. To support the rights and democratic will of the people I serve, unswayed by inappropriate commercial, career or political pressures.

5. To protect and uphold the principles of rule of law, respect for all people, valuing and protecting human rights, liberty, freedom of expression and democracy.

6. To respect and uphold the principles of equal opportunity in all matters of public office and for all the people served by me.

7. To respect and uphold appropriate protection of the countryside and environment in the area I serve and the world in general.

8. Not to misuse public funded resources nor gain personal financial benefit or gifts in kind other than those, which are intended to be passed over in their entirety to the benefit of the broader community with no gain to myself, family, or friends.

9. In respect of above I will accept no new remunerated directorships or consultancy roles after taking up public office except roles directly benefiting the community and not adversely affecting my input to, or performance in public service.

10. To provide regular and open access to the people I serve to make full use of my services and to hold me to account. This could be in the form of regular and confidential surgeries, confidential 1 to 1 meetings or public forums to meet the needs of the people served.

11. To uphold the principles of freedom of information and openness/ honesty at all times and encourage others to scrutinise inappropriate activities of public concern.

12. Be committed to working within a ethical and moral framework in public office to promote and deliver benefits to people both locally and in the wider world community.

I had hoped that as the code of conduct for MPs had been sent to her twice over the previous few years that she would hopefully influence the Prime Minister to introduce such a code and seek to prevent the MP expense abuse scandal, which followed in 2009. However it was not to be as events turned out. As it happened the only thing she commented on was the prophecy of mine made years before relating to Tony Blair and John Prescott. I did of course get the detail mixed up when my logic kicked in and told me that out of the two men Prescott would probably not be the first choice of the two to seduce any blonde with his charm and good looks. As it turned out I was wrong and John Prescott obviously had the appeal to the woman featured later in the media. I also had a thought that perhaps my replies from Cherie that Sunday were actually from her secretary or PA perhaps and queried that. The same day I sent the following email:

Subject: Thanks

Just got back from an Italian restaurant with my wife and daughter and had an uncanny thought....How do I know its you replying and not some Scouse PA or spook at Cheltenham GCHQ . Signing off for the next few months or more.

She got back to me five hours later with a reply suggesting that only she would be around at 9.30 on a Sunday evening. Well there it was. The good lady was on her own perhaps working on her book or diary on her day off, the poor thing. All the staff, servants and maids at Chequers must have retired for the day. A few months later I wrote to her about a psychic experience I thought she may have been interested in. I also told her of my concerns for her favourite charity, a hospice with two care homes she had supported from her school days and of which one was now Vice President. As it happened the hospice care home in question was closed down two and a half years later. But that is another story. At the time of my email the Israelis were bombing the Lebanon and causing death and destruction to many innocent civilians. I believed the UK Government should be more critical of the Israeli strategy whereas tens of thousands of civilians were suffering badly by what seemed indiscriminate bombing and shelling. Jack Straw had raised serious concerns about the unnecessary death and destruction on the civilian population but the Prime Minister seemed generally muted on the effects of the Israeli invasion. On 30th July 2006 I emailed the following:

Subject: Jospice and stuff

Dear Ms Booth

'Stuff':

A few months ago in a Liverpool cafe a high flying corporate adviser was asking my advice about different paths she had to consider in her life. I suggested that she should follow her inner urge/follow her heart etc,. She went to pull out a book in her briefcase and before it appeared in view I said page 78. We had both not read the book and I had never heard of it before. She opened the page and the first paragraph - page 78 replicated to the word what I had just advised her. The book was The Cosmic Ordering Service. Whether I subscribe to the book's theories I don't yet know. She wrote in the book to record that event and gave it to me as she said she would buy another copy. Sometime later she told me she decided to follow her heart for her sake and that of her new family. With world events and pressures your role is clearly more demanding than glamorous and life moves so fast. I hope you follow your heart and inner urge in life's decision making, whereas the voice of logic should not always prevail. Perhaps you are facing some cross-roads and soul searching in this summer of 2006?

Jospice matters:

Strictly private & confidential -   For information

My colleague and I have been doing pro bono support work for the Jospice for a few years and in particular trying to keep the Health & Safety Exec/Care Standards Commission from coming down too hard on Hettinga House, Ormskirk. (Further'crunch' meeting August). I was v concerned to hear a view expressed by the General Manager to myself recently that it may 'be just as easy to close down Ormskirk Jospice and sell the assets for £7 - £800,000 if things got difficult'. I have stressed to him the importance of being positive and entrepreneurial/carrying forward Father O Leary's faith based legacy etc. Nearly three years ago I suggested that to protect the future of Ormskirk the Jospice should engage in talks with property developers etc to secure by a mutual agreement a realisation of some of the 6 acre site with either a refurbished building or a purpose built new hospice building in the grounds. Albeit at this late stage talks are now underway with developers but the future still looks uncertain with Ormskirk staff morale rock bottom. A new support group has been established in Ormskirk. I and others will continue to promote a positive and proactive solution to secure Ormskirk's future. I have suggested direct talks with the new Primary Care Trust, a revived media campaign, awareness raising to decision makers etc. (New research - West Lancs has a shortage of hospice beds).

Will work to secure shared aims for the Jospice survival in Ormskirk.

Lastly I share Jack Straw's view on the middle east crisis... I wonder how many other people do?

Best wishes
Bill

She thanked me for my comments and what we were trying to do for the hospice. No comment was made on the psychic experience I had experienced, nor my concerns for the future of the hospice. As Vice-President of that Jospice she did not choose to engage with me directly on the challenges facing the hospice or the proposed strategy we were putting together. I realised she was indeed a very busy lady but I was saddened that considering her role past and present in the hospice that she did not seek more information from me and other stakeholders working at the Ormskirk hospice to secure its future. Cherie did not respond either to my comments about Jack Straw and his views on the Israeli invasion of the Lebanon. Later that year Cherie was again in the media after someone complained about her allegedly touching the back of a 17 male, who had made a rabbit ears gesture by raising his index and middle fingers behind her head.

This allegedly happened during her visit to a national school sports event on September 9, 2006 in Glasgow. The Scottish Strathclyde police was reported to state it has been established that no incident took place after completing a probe that involved six detectives responding to a complaint from officials from the Child Protection in Sport Unit. Yet again a stupid allegation against her, about, which I wrote to her September 17th 2006 offering support. The what do you call a scouser in a suit comment is a Liverpool joke, with the answer being - the accused or the defend

Dear Cherie
So sorry to hear of this week's pathetic 'political correctness' inquisition resulting from a harmless situation. The AOL news today has this following instant survey result:
Child protection laws are good 2,170   8%
Political correctness has gone too far 25,918   92%

Perhaps The Mail On Sunday should have devoted two and half pages to what the world should be supporting/implementing in Darfur rather than to this ridiculous so called 'story'. Hoping that the next half of your life mission leaves you free you to pursue what is in your heart as a person who knows her own mind and has not got any time to waste on such unwarranted distractions. 'What do you call a scouser in a suit' scenario perhaps?

Best wishes
Bill

She commented on how ridiculous the issue was and said that perhaps our paths may cross as she was in Liverpool the next day. I wasn't sure whether our paths would cross so I sent a joke email about her meeting me for a babycham in a Liverpool city centre pub of which she had the good sense to decline. As Liverpool, my beloved city was Capital Of Culture City in 2008 I headed the email accordingly. Many years ago in my twenties I used to sing with live groups in Liverpool and beyond and felt I could support her Beatles song/singing attempt as filmed during her visit to China some years before.

Subject: Liverpool Capital of Singing.

Have a good time in Liverpool tomorrow. Pity you can't relax, eg go to an all day karaoke pub in the city centre I know and unwind. We could have done a few songs after a babycham and pint of bitter perhaps. Love is all around - by Wet Wet Wet perhaps, or even Yesterday by the Beatles. I have sung in China - also to college students ('Unchained Melody') sometime before your world famous performance and in Turkey a few weeks ago on a Gullet. Just before they chucked me overboard. Enjoy your visit amongst friends.

Best wishes
Bill

She assured me she would have a good time in Liverpool. A month or so later, in October 2006 in a moment of madness perhaps I sent her a copy of a book chapter I had written detailing events witnessed by many credible people. They were of so called psychic happenings that had happened in my life time as an identical twin etc. I knew she had a great interest in this field as around 60% of the population do and thought that some feed-back from her could be helpful to me in various ways. I also asked her how her new book was coming on as I for some time could visualise her burning the midnight oil sitting by her computer working on the book framework. Well, we all have to pay the (many) mortgage(s) don't we?

Subject: Book Chapter?

Dear Ms Booth

I am writing a book about Psychic stuff etc you may wish to read (this chapter attached) - to send you to sleep on one plane journey or so. I know you are v busy so if it goes in the shredder I will understand. I still believe you are facing a big decision making event in your life so as the chapter says follow your heart/inner voice and not the voice of logic. (How is your new book/diaries progressing......?)

Best wishes

Bill

She replied saying she would read the chapter with interest, but she was apparently to busy too give me any feedback and it probably went in the waste-bin. Previous emails by me had communicated clearly my despair at the immense suffering in Darfur whilst the world watched and waited for the United Nations to get its act together. I still believed that Tony Blair as world statesman had the opportunity to be more proactive in brokering ways to end the suffering. I also believed that I should keep trying to influence Cherie to influence him to seek ways to resolve the conflict with international pressure and as a peacemaker following their Christian beliefs. As ex MP Martin Bell once said politics was too important to be left to politicians or words to that effect. Hence my waging peace proposal, which has its namesake in an organisation based in London. They were with limited resources actively waging peace around the world. Just before Christmas in 2006 I sent the following email:

Subject: Waging Peace

Dear Ms Booth

The greatest gift of the Prime Ministers's political legacy to this world would be the ending of the genocide and inhumanity in Darfur. Diplomacy and political dialogue hasn't worked. We await tough talk about sanctions etc but in the meantime families, just as we have, are broken, young and old murdered, women raped and children made orphans and homeless. We look forward to our safe Christmas and family love whilst others weep and feel the pain. In May 2005 you mentioned seeking a UN Security Council agreement. A further 18 months of politics has allowed thousands of people to die in the meantime. The Prime Minister is only human and cannot work miracles, but he can perhaps go that one step further and if in doing so he saves the life of one innocent in Darfur then he will be blessed. Pre-Iraq invasion in February 2003 I wrote to you and suggested that the Prime Minister fly out to Iraq to seek a solution acceptable to the UK and USA to avoid loss of lives. Unknown to myself at the time Sir Richard Branson had arranged to fly to Iraq with Nelson Mandela for the same objective but was stopped by the launch of the bombing campaign.

Cannot the Prime Minister fly out to Sudan with someone as a broker/negotiator, like Mandela and affect a lasting solution to the genocide? Focusing world opinion via the PM in dialogue with those complicit with genocide may mean a breakthrough. Spelling out in strong terms the effect on the Government of the Sudan if they continue to ignore the ongoing carnage is essential? In February 2003 I also wrote to you and said that solving global problems was part of the PM's destiny. For him to leave office without a solution to Darfur inspired/driven by him would be such a wasted opportunity, a waste of the lives of innocents. We are all equal in this world and I would like to at least try through you for a better world. As Christians it must be right to forgo political constraints and protocol and do what the heart tells is the right thing to do. Those families in Darfur are searching the sky above for solutions, which only the influential and powerful can facilitate. The old approach hasn't worked - something new and effective is needed urgently as we look forward to our Christmas. This Christmas can we not see our Prime Minister waging peace in Darfur?

Best wishes

Bill

She was of course kind enough to give me some encouragement in her reply by saying it was a good idea and she would pass it on. However time will tell whether Tony Blair's new role in the world as Middle East Peace Envoy after leaving Downing Street will contribute to peace in Darfur and other places. What transpired was that Tony Blair did not take the initiative that Christmas as a peace envoy nor did he demonstrate he was the star of peace and hope many including myself were hoping to see. He did not visit Darfur and Sudan and I believe he went off as guest to a holiday in the Caribbean instead to top up his sun-tan. In January 2007 I received an email from Dame Helena Kennedy.

The email was about the dangers facing our democracy because of falling standards in public life, planned political manipulation on freedom of information, cronyism in the House of Lords, plans to extend police powers to lock up suspects for longer periods etc. In the consultation process I had contributed some policy ideas to an initiative called the *Power Commission*, which was reviewing the state of the British democratic process. Helena Kennedy QC and Labour Peer was Chair of the enquiry. She said:

Politics and government are increasingly in the hands of privileged elites, as if democracy has run out of steam......Too often, citizens are being evicted from decision making - rarely asked to get involved and rarely listened to. As a result, they see no point in voting, joining a party or engaging with formal politics.

Really good ideas I thought, which I forwarded to Cherie. There was some media speculation about her becoming an MP. I just wanted to get a reaction - which I got two hours later:

Subject: Fwd: The POWER Inquiry launch of a new campaign

Dear Ms Booth
For your interest. Do you fancy standing as an MP on these issues one day?
Best wishes
Bill

(Somewhat Sad ex Blairite)

Well she made it quite clear she had no intention of standing as an MP. How about Special Ambassador to the United Nations in human rights perhaps I thought. Well time will tell. I was not to write to her for four months or so after probably pissing her off somewhat. She has since gone on to tour the world speaking in the main about the rights of women.

11

No 10 JOURNAL - VICE PRESIDENT CHERIE BLAIR

For over a decade colleagues and I had been providing free advice and support to various hospices, charities and individuals. We formed a small charity called The Business Trust for this purpose. A local hospice charity we had supported for a few years - Jospice, had two sites, one in Cherie's child-hood town Crosby and the smaller site in Ormskirk, Lancashire some eight miles away. Cherie had been a life-long supporter of the Jospice - near Liverpool and accepted a position as Vice-President of the charity. I had supported a Jospice fund-raising business lunch in January 2005. She as charity Vice-President and guest speaker introduced a political statement into the event by announcing to the audience about the £x million or so the Labour Government had made available for hospices across the country. Hospices were still vastly under-funded by the government even after that announcement. In stark contrast MPs were still well funded though as it later turned out in 2009.

Eighteen months later her Jospice management and majority of Trustees proposed the closure of the smaller twelve bedded Hospice in Ormskirk and disposal by sale to a commercial purchaser. This was to provide revenue and to safeguard the (head office based) Hospice in Mrs Blair's childhood town. I, with thousands of other supporters opposed the closure plan. I was especially against the closure as there was a shortage of end of life care beds in the region and one long term coma patient in particular was to lose her home. Alison aged 36, a mother of three children had been lovingly cared for there for about five years. Her room was like a family bedroom with family photographs and regular visits from the family. The nursing staff were brilliant and provided Alison's every need with great love and care. I believed passionately that the hospice had with support a viable long term future and could generate income to support its survival and growth. After examining the accounts, getting a specialist opinion from a city insolvency accounting practice along with a professional appraisal of the buildings and land assets, I was even more convinced of its future potential. I and others, including professional accountants, building experts, fundraisers had felt that closure could definitely be avoided.

I queried the way costs were allocated across the two sites, reviewed the business plan strategy, looked at the strengths, weaknesses, opportunities etc and believed the Hospice was viable if innovative commercial solutions were implemented and supported. Some senior key members of the mainly elderly trustees in the charity confided in me and said they could not read the accounts presented to them by the hospice team. That was of great concern to me. Ultimately the will and passion to safeguard and develop Ormskirk with the proposed innovative business and community support on offer was not taken up by the charity trustees. After the proposed closure plans were released to the local media, Granada TV visited the hospice and filmed for a news story. A campaign group headed by myself and the hospice matron was formed following the growing opposition to the planned closure from the local community.

Because of my long-standing voluntary involvement in the hospice, I with three colleagues was invited to the Jospice reception at 10 Downing Street,

May 2nd 2007. That last visit proved to be educational in many ways. A film company was at No 10 covering the reception and Cherie in particular for a programme shown on BBC TV later that month. I later discovered the programme was called *The Real Cherie*. BBC Presenter Fiona Bruce approached me inside No 10 with a cameraman and asked my opinion of the Blairs. I replied that Cherie had done so much to support charitable causes and that I would be very interested to see the next chapter of their lives unfolding with the planned roll-out of the now media reported Blair Foundation(s). I said that we would just have to wait and see what impact it had.

This concept it then seemed was now underway and web domain names had been registered for the foundation. Off-camera I asked Fiona Bruce whether she knew anything about the closure plans for one of the two hospices of Cherie's charity. My aim was to point out that all guests that day, including some local Labour MPs, were drinking wine and eating canapés and having a jolly time when one of the two long established local hospices was getting closed down and not a word was said about its fate and effect on the staff, patients and community. Fiona Bruce didn't really seem too interested and the programme went out a few weeks later without a mention of the closure. Everything appeared hunky-dory to the viewers in The Real Cherie programme.

I, for one, on principle did not drink the wine that evening, nor eat the canapés or join in the party spirit whilst terminally ill patients effectively faced eviction/relocation from Vice-President Cherie's favourite hospice because of alleged reasons of funding. Strangely enough at that time although the charity owned the two hospice sites, which where 30 minutes apart by car I was told that neither the Matron nor any of the staff in the threatened hospice had been invited to Downing Street for the high profile charity bash. In view of the fact that staff from the co-provider Crosby hospice were guests at No 10 I thought that failure to include a few of their long serving colleagues from the second hospice was disgraceful. Long-standing loyal and caring nurses and support staff with years of service facing redundancy felt they were the poor relations because of the failure to invite them.

They had also alleged that many of the charity Trustees (and Vice President Cherie) had allegedly not visited them over the previous years. A meeting at No 10 or visit from their Vice President would have given them the opportunity to put their case to Cherie who was it seems a well-known advocate of people's rights. Alison as the long term coma patient who was effectively losing her home could have benefitted with an advocate to represent her rights. Our hospice is closing our hospice was the reality actually underway whilst Cherie and friends laughed and sang an old school song with the cameras rolling. Inspiration, fighting talk and support from one of the most influential women in the world to save the threatened hospice was not evident to those affected in Ormskirk. A wish not realised that day, nor evident during the campaign. Perhaps she did contribute much behind the scenes to prevent the closure. If she did myself and all the staff of the doomed hospice were totally unaware of it. One fiftieth of the joint earnings from the Blair's planned book sales and world stage income would have saved the Catholic originated hospice and provided a base for securing a viable future.

A few years before I had arranged a business lunch event in Liverpool with Cherie as guest speaker. I invited a teenage girl to the lunch who was living with a lifelong disability. A disability, which did not suppress her strong spirit or lovely smiling face. Cherie offered the teenager some inspirational words and told her that she could be what she wanted in life. As a Christian I was extremely sad and disappointed that such inspirational words with a can-do attitude did not manifest to support the local campaigners who had viable business and care focussed solutions on offer to avert closure. Positive actions were demonstrated publicly by celebrities Christine Hamilton and Jon Culshaw in supporting our campaign. Sadly despite my pleas and presenting the case for saving the hospice there was no public show of support or encouragement from Hospice Vice President Cherie Blair. Blair's legacy - Tony's that is, was notably absent in this case. The failure by ten years of his leadership to address the funding gap for care of the dying in this country to me was a failed legacy for such a high profile Christian who could authorise £billions to be spent on waging war.

By not addressing under-funding of hospices with adequate public monies that had been a contributing factor in the closure decision for Ormskirk. The revelations some years later about the parliamentary scandal of MP expenses and allowances had shown that public monies were squandered by self-serving MPs when hospices around the UK were struggling to survive. New Politics - New priorities for directing funding. Booth's legacy I believe was not to publicly support the practical options available for keeping the hospice going and this was described by me in emails to her. If I, as a Christian, had the power as Blair had I would have at least funded half the costs of UK hospice care from a miniscule increase in taxation on say tobacco or alcohol. If I was in Cherie's position again as Vice-President I would have hoped I could have found at least a few hours to visit the threatened hospice service at Ormskirk to talk to the affected staff, patients and meet with those having a strategy for the future. If I were in her position I would have utilised my resources and influence in a high profile effort to preserve the home and loving support for the dying and their families.

I emailed Cherie a detailed analysis of the current situation and potential for future sustainability of the hospice if the management board support and will to save the hospice was demonstrated. To back this up on 3rd May 2007.I sent her a You Tube DVD produced by my brother showing the hospice facilities and interviews with some of the staff and family members. I was constantly reminded that she had never visited the Ormskirk site in her capacity as Vice-President and that she had never afforded the local staff the opportunity to meet or hear their case.

Subject: No 10 Jospice Visit/Storm Clouds over Ormskirk Hospice Closure

Dear Cherie
Strictly Private and Confidential.

I have been periodically supportive/critical of (policies) in my emails to you since 2002 when my letter of support for you was published in the Daily Mail during the Foster rubbish. For some weeks now I have intended to send you my final email before you move on from your historic home. That is to thank you for your timely replies - even when I have been both supportive of issues and also highly critical of Govt policy. Thank you for finding the time over the years and considering my thoughts on a wide range of issues. In the future I hope your new found 'freedom' allows you to follow your heart on to your destiny and next phase of your life mission. Storm clouds are gathering around the recently publicised intended closure of Hettinga House (Ormskirk). The many 'hawks'and the 'doves' fighting the closure are gearing up and it is inevitable that local media (Granada/L/pool Echo etc) will escalate up to national media coverage. In my opinion (advising businesses and charities for decades and supported by professional opinion and public good will) there is a positive and sustainable future for Ormskirk.

The reality is that with the right approach, professional help, passion and a will to succeed that Hettinga has a future. Last week I held the hand and stroked the brow of a lovely 36 year old mother of three whose home now is a room in Hettinga. With her Mum at my side and the Matron with us I said a prayer for her and family with the 'closure'/uncertainty around it impacting on so many good people. Eight months ago I wrote to you about my concerns about Ormskirk. You spoke so eloquently about Father O' Leary and his ongoing legacy in the care provided by the Jospice. His approach as you know so well was: 'Can Do and whilst we breathe there is hope'. I and other professionals, families and staff strongly believe Ormskirk has a sustainable future. Have you/other senior stakeholders been briefed with all the facts and options or provided with such a compelling/substantive financial case for closing the hospice?

Some facts: (with detail/independent professional opinion to support these facts available)

(1) The Echo newspaper stated that the building is 'not fit for purpose'. That is not the case. The building is sound and can be upgraded. Neither the care standards authorities nor the health & safety exec to my

knowledge are saying patients cannot be cared for - or that the service must cease.

(2) The accounts for both sites are merged into overall accounts. Initial review by accounts specialists and initial review by company turn around/insolvency experts are saying that there seems no compelling case for closure. (currently awaiting full feed-back on the subject matter).

(3) There appears no detailed/independently audited split of costs for both sites, to indicate that Ormskirk is a drain on total resources. In contrast as most of the staff in Hettinga take below market rate salaries with low management costs the cost per bed/ patient care may actually be lower than Thornton. (proviso - fair share of appropriate overhead costs etc).

(4) The £40 million govt capital grant scheme to hospices was administered by Help The Hospices, whose Q&A Guidance - Oct 2006 clearly stated that the Dept of Health 'expectation was that grants will range between £25000 and £250000. You may apply for more than £250000 but you should note that multi-million pound applications are unlikely to succeed'

NB: The total application by the Jospice was in excess of £two million and therefore extremely unlikely that the capital grant application of £1.7 million for Ormskirk would even be considered.

(5) Multiple grant applications were actually encouraged by the Dept of Health. Therefore if the Jospice also applied for say Ormskirk refurbishment grants etc (eg Options A, B, C etc for Ormskirk) for say £300,000 - £500,000 (plus Thornton application) the

application would at least have been in with a chance and Ormskirk's situation strengthened.

(6) There was a lottery funded grant subject to application for community buildings initiative of around £250000, which could have been applied using a creative approach for widening the community use in Hettinga, eg use of cottages there, bereavement/holistic services for the community and income generation. (eg The Hale Clinic approach ???).

I spoke to the lottery who said such a scheme described would have been strongly considered. Problem being the Jospice have missed the deadline - 30th April.

The point being had this funding provision been successfully applied for, this could have been another potential income source for both capital and revenue income generation for future years. (Jospice regretfully missed this potential opportunity for funds).

(7) West Lancashire supporters and stakeholders attended various meetings at Hettinga over the last year with various ideas and resources proposed for Ormskirk's future. The directive given by the General Manager was basically to leave things with him. Myself and all other stakeholders only learned of the closure plan via local newspapers. When the Gen Manager was asked to hold a meeting to discuss the issues he said "he had nothing to put on the agenda/nothing to discuss" and said he would not be holding a meeting.

(8) Without adding to all the detail above there are solutions supported by professionals to secure the Jospice services and Hettinga in particular. We must not allow this wonderful service to close.

On 12th December 2002 you wrote to me and said:

'Thank you so much I appreciate and need your support'.

With respect, the patients, wonderful staff and families now need your influential support with your role and passion for these services and to keep Father O' Leary's legacy alive and blossoming.

On Tuesday night before I travelled down to No 10 I looked out to Ainsdale beach to see a beautiful night sky with one amazing brilliant star (or planet) to focus my gaze on and a brilliant full moon behind me. I thought of the young mum in Ormskirk and her family who was not as lucky as me/my family to enjoy 'normal' life.

We must not allow Ormskirk to close and I and others cannot accept that the building is unfit for purpose nor that solutions do not exist. It is inevitable that this issue will develop and move from a regional to a national news story and this is a matter of regret that it should ever have reached this stage.

We can go forward but the will has got to be there, laced with some of the passion of the founder, combined with business led solutions. Thanks for your time and your hospitality yesterday.

Best wishes

PS: I have taken the liberty of sending by post a short DVD of Ormskirk Hospice produced by my twin brother with the staff/families at Hettinga House. I hope you can view it.

The DVD was put on You Tube and presented an appeal from the heart by the matron of the hospice. I don't know if Cherie ever viewed the film. She certainly did not comment on the words expressed. She did respond briefly by saying that she knew a senior manager at the hospice head office well and the opinion was that it is impossible to save the hospice. I was extremely disappointed by the response and a month or so later on 9th June 2007 I replied with my analysis of the Blair years followed by another appeal to help secure the hospice.

Subject: Jospice, Blair - Booth Foundation

Dear Mrs Blair

I have written you about 20 emails over the last five years, met you and your husband on occasions over the last decade. You on your part have had the courtesy to reply to all my thoughts and comments in those emails. Thoughts and opinions both supportive and at times critical of policies and outcomes. In this historic office opportunities entrusted to you and the Prime Minister I believe that you have both sadly lost something precious along the way. Decisions or policies often presented in an arena of 'tough decision making' and self belief. Decisions, however often remote from the impact of the reality of that decision or path taken. Decisions affecting fellow mankind with no looking back, or even forward looking it seems.

Both of you have had great power and influence entrusted in you. It could have been a decade of greatness, it was a decade of great loss in many ways. On a macro level this world is not a safer place, nor a more democratic place with 'Blairism' but on the contrary the 'Blair Legacy' leaves us all with more fears, more concerns and less freedom than in May 1997. Your heart must concur with me even though your logic may rush to defend the outcomes of the last decade. A successful economy founded on a Tory economic base saw many more billions spent, but badly invested on public services. A 'feel good factor' by the many not a counter-balance to the mismanagement by Government of 'initiatives', which have ended in waste and doubtful outcomes, nationally and globally. Tonight I watched Sir Bob Geldof delivering his powerful analysis of the PM's 'goodbye' G8 Summit. Sir Bob's passionate analysis was statesmanlike, frank and accurate, which exposed the impotence of this Government/The PM on the world stage in influencing the rich nations to assist the poor nations.

The PM had fine words to say but failed to leave a legacy for us all to be proud of. His legacy of 'intervention' has failed Darfur, failed Zimbabwe and many other countries and poor peoples around the world. As a Christian I find it incredible that ten years on in this country, children's hospices only receive on average about 6% of their funding from Government sources, with adult hospices about 33%. At No 10, 2nd May 2007, I drank water, others drank wine and 'canapéd', you sang with your ex school chums, announced proudly to the camera your Government's grant for Crosby Hospice new chapel etc, but you failed to say one word about the announced closure of Jospice 'sister' hospice in Ormskirk. Good people, Christians and non-Christians, are fighting the battle to save one of your hospices, which it seems you have not visited for some time.

For example in this case is the PM/you supporting with your heart and indeed soul a campaign/actions for funding/securing the care of the dying? If not for the hospice you are Vice-President of then the rest of the hospice network? The reality it seems is demonstrated by the funding levels against the waste of public monies elsewhere. Independent analysis shows there is no compelling financial reason to close Ormskirk down and if the will is there it can be developed for future generations. I personally cannot understand your readiness to give up hope and not even try to find a solution with a wider support network.

At least MP Hazel Blears and other MPs/Ministers were willing to join public protests recently and support stakeholders when their local NHS hospital services were facing closure. Sometimes I feel annoyed, to put it mildly, and other times feel sorry for what you have both seemed to have lost in your last decade in positions of power and influence. Three and a half years ago I wrote and said that: 'with respect, if things dont change the PM may leave office considered as a good PM, but will if things don't change will miss that wonderful opportunity to be considered as a great PM' Four years ago today I suggested to you the 'Blair/Booth Foundation' for the common good across the globe. However it would appear that based on your lack of positive action to support me and others to secure Ormskirk Hospice then perhaps you may wish to review your life mission. The Blair legacy, if judged by me and many others, a Blair 'Disciple' for half Tony's 'reign', is sadly lacking in sustainable good deeds, strengthened democracy, peace initiatives as the current facts suggest.

Perhaps people like me amongst the millions who had faith, and the millions around the world who had hope, will say 'well at least they tried, but perhaps should have gone one step further and not left office with a vision, battered and unfulfilled'. It may be water off a ducks back to you both in your future

201

roles/earning capacity, however the bottom line of this last decade as measured by achievements is not a legacy I for one would be proud of. In the meantime I and many others will, without your help, work to secure the future care of Alison, 36 year old mum of three whose home for five years has been Ormskirk Jospice and a place where we celebrated her birthday a few weeks ago. Of course you would not be aware of her or her kind, loving family. Perhaps you should have taken time out to meet her and her family, the staff of your hospice before you formed an opinion on the reasons to close this wonderful hospice down.

Bill

She wrote back and confirmed that in her opinion, without any discussion with myself or the Ormskirk team that the hospice could not be saved. The reality was that it of course it could have been saved and celebrity Christine Hamilton sent me a letter supporting that opinion. When I gave Christine the feedback from Cherie she sent me an email expressing her dismay and said amongst other things *..not only is that an extraordinary statement from the Vice President of the hospice, it is also defeatist and plain wrong. Of course It can be saved and with enough public determination and effort it will be.* Shortly afterwards impressionist and comedian Jon Culshaw raised £10,000 on TV show *Who wants to be a millionaire* specifically for the Ormskirk hospice. If there is a will there is a way is what many people said to me.

The will had to be from the top down. One of the difficulties faced by those opposing the closure was that some of the Hospice Trustees did not have the skills or experience in analysing or questioning financial and management accounts of the charity. Some Trustees including an influential Trustee with a professional career admitted to me that she could not read or understand accounts. My very last email to Cherie 26th June 2007 was the only one she never replied to. This was sent in the Blair's last few days in Downing Street. I put in the title - the real Cherie.

Subject: Farewell - the real Cherie

Dear Cherie

Just a final note to say farewell. You will not have to endure my supportive or indeed pain in the butt critical correspondence ever again. I also write that I feel it is not the real Cherie who has been replying to me re: the hospice closure issue but perhaps another person is replying? Someone who has been delegated that task but has not done his/her homework.

I say this as I believe that it is difficult to comprehend that one of the finest legal minds and eminent human rights 'champion' is perhaps only relying on a phone call summary of the hospice closure reasons without being willing to see all the supportive evidence to keep Ormskirk going. For example Ormskirk does operate, as indeed Crosby does in a breakeven/surplus financial situation - it most definitely can continue and be developed if the will exists and independent experts are afforded time to assist .

The Real Cherie: Crosby girl with a heart.

I saw you at the Crowne Plaza lunch in 2005 telling/inspiring ...... the young cerebral palsy sufferer with her Mum that she 'could achieve anything in this world'. The same inspirational Cherie is not coming across now in your willingness to accept closure and the loss of a home for a mum of three being nursed at Hettinga House Hospice. Her family are poor and live in Kirkby and have no resources to fight for her human rights. Myself and other professional/volunteers will not give in. It is so sad that this hospice if closed will be a negative aspect of the Blair legacy/Govt funding failures. May I say from me there has been no personal antagonism against you or Mr Blair rather an analytical presentation of the facts from a one time Blair 'Disciple' and someone who has been a professional adviser to the public, political, private and not for profit sector most of my working life. From a Christian perspective, as a sinner more than a saint, I do believe that perhaps something special has been lost along the way, albeit we are all human and make mistakes, make the wrong decisions along the way.

I honestly believe that in pursuit of wealth or power insulated from real people that you will both never find true happiness and contentment in your lives. I have, however, enjoyed my visits to Downing Street etc and experiencing the historic Blair journey since 1995 through the valleys and over high mountains, and stormy weather and rainbows as it were. I do hope the new chapters in your life/Blair Foundation etc are written for the good of many and not for the few.

Bill

By a strange coincidence that evening, on the day my email headed 'The Real Cherie' was sent to Cherie it was announced that a programme featuring the Prime Minister's wife was to be shown the following Wednesday night. Its title was The Real Cherie. (Also by another strange coincidence my mention of rainbow in my last email was to be somewhat prophetic.) A rainbow appeared over Tony Blair's constituency during the Blair's farewell visit, much to the amusement of the assembled world media). It was also reported in the media that The BBC was to spend an estimated £100,000 of licence-payers money on Cherie's documentary. Myself as a TV Licence payer was of the opinion that it was a waste of money considering the fact that my interview with BBC's Fiona Bruce pointing out that a hospice was being closed down was not broadcast. That at least should have been aired. My email clearly expressed my strongly felt opinions and belief that perhaps with Cherie's high profile support we could have mounted a pro- active campaign to save the hospice for the community.

Cherie was of course a very busy person. Cherie was reported in the media some months later to be concerned with the rights of people in care homes. It was reported that she believed that elderly residents of care homes did not have the same rights as prisoners in UK jails. This opinion relates to a Law Lords ruling in 2007 stating that people in independent care homes were outside the scope of the Human Rights Act. It was reported that care standards legislation does not cover all negligent situations nor does it prevent a care home from evicting a resident. It was also reported in the New York Times July 18th 2006 that Cherie Blair offers legal help to rights groups in Russia.

It was also reported that after a G8 Summit meeting attended by President Bush, Tony Blair and other world leaders that Ms Blair made the offer while meeting privately with several of the (human rights) organisations.........Two participants in the meeting said that Ms Blair told them British Lawyers could offer assistance in appeals to the European Court Of Human Rights and that she seemed sincere in her concerns. At Christmas 2007 I received in the post a glossy newsletter from the hospice with front page smiley photograph of Cherie Blair – offering Christmas greetings from our Vice President Cherie Blair.

On the back page of the newsletter was an announcement from the General Manager of the hospice about the closure of the Ormskirk site. He stated that in the event all remaining patients had passed away or (in line with their relatives request) been transferred to Jospice Thornton. He also stated that the closure was a casualty of the failure of successive governments to fund hospices properly. His observation about the patients passing away was I felt rather insensitive and that many, many more terminally ill people would have benefited from a loving, caring environment in the beautiful surroundings that the hospice offered.

In July 2010 I looked at the Charities Commission accounts for the hospice for the year ending March 2009. There was a statement in the accounts, which said....*the receipt of sale proceeds for the former site of Hettinga House*, (The former hospice) which produced a gain of £737,000 in the value of a fixed asset. So it appeared that that net gain resulted from the property sale of a beautiful green belt six-acre site with a large structurally sound detached house, woods, a detached cottage and outbuildings minutes from the town centre, rail station and ten minutes from a motorway link.

When I read the accounts I just could not relate what I thought the value of the property was with what was finally agreed to by the board of trustees for the hospice. My concerns raised with Cherie in July 2006 about a selling off the large house, cottages and six acres of gardens as the Ormskirk site was for £7-800,000 was actually realised it seemed. As a key asset of the charity the purchase price of that substantial property with all its potential was clearly a once in a lifetime bargain for the eventual purchaser even in a time of economic uncertainty. In August 2010 I visited the Ormskirk hospice, which had gates front and back installed like something from the Berlin wall era. Massive padlocks and access denied to the beautiful grounds. I wondered how those people whose loved ones ashes which were located at various points around the hospice grounds felt when their place of memory and resting place were denied everyday access as in past years. People had also paid for trees to be planted in the grounds in memory of their loved ones. I presume those trees were replanted to accessible locations elsewhere?

As for Cherie and politics I can't really see her getting proactively involved in political activity and perhaps as ongoing Vice President of the remaining hospice will be the closest political sounding office she will hold. Time will tell though and I can only envisage Tony and her taking different paths in life. On 27th June 2007 they both left Downing Street with Cherie having the last word with the waiting media in the street. She said she wouldn't miss them. Well not until she needs some publicity about her human rights crusade or other campaigns. In the meantime the proceeds from her book sales were quoted in the media from £1 to £1.5 million. I'm sure if that income is realised then it will provide some monies for the good of the many. Hospice care perhaps? On 4th June 2008 I again met the first lady of UK politics. She was in Liverpool to promote her new book and I popped along to the city's historic Bluecoat centre where she was giving a talk and an interview with local Radio Merseyside. She talked about her childhood and said there was a shortage of money as her dad did not send money home and she was looked after by her dads mother when six weeks old. She was however immensely proud of her dad and mentioned that he appeared in the musical O Calcutta. Regarding her professional life she, as a Barrister, took cases under the cab rank rule including cases against the government of which her husband was Prime Minister.

She said she had one case opposing the smoking ban arguing an infringement of human rights. She mentioned that Tony Blair whilst in Paris had a premonition that something was about to happen just before the party leader John Smith died in 1994 from a heart attack. She was asked about the story in her book that her son Leo was conceived whilst staying at the Queen's home, Balmoral.

She said she did not give gory details about her sex life as such in the book. Cherie made a point of saying that world leaders are human like the rest of us with a job to do although it was strange that a girl from 15 Ferndale Road, Liverpool should end up in the White House talking to actor Harrison Ford and the US president. She said her left of centre politics was influenced by her faith, a belief in God and she had those things in common with Tony Blair. She said she had had some criticism for making her husband look like a human being and that most politicians have a mission to make a difference.

She said that criticism puts a lot of people off going into politics. In response to a question about the House of Parliament being dominated by lawyers and barristers she said that was a sweeping statement as lawyers were used to presenting arguments. She did suggest that greater diversity was needed in the House with more women, minorities etc. It was interesting that she believed that politics was a full time role and that it couldn't be done part-time. She went on to say that it would be nice to be able to walk across Liverpool and that she felt immensely proud of Liverpool and proud to be a Liverpudlian. Straight after the audience with Cherie I met her and she asked me what I wanted her to write in her new book. I suggested pain in the arse emailer etc.

Her reply was well you were nice most of the time or words to that effect. She wrote in her book *To Bill my email* friend and passed it over to me and I beat a hasty retreat to meet a friend. As it happened our paths were to cross again early in 2010, again in Liverpool, our hometown. A place of humour, warmth and bolshie scousers like Cherie and I perhaps.

12

NEW LABOUR'S LEGACY

Labour's election victory in the heady days of May 1997 seemed to re-energise the rest of the country with widespread optimism for the following years, hope for the new millennium. I and millions of New Labour converts genuinely thought that 43 year old Tony Blair had the passion, the ability and drive to make a positive difference in our world. I shared many of his stated aims as countless others did and warmed to his boyish smile, his aura of political sincerity and his stated belief in social justice. Like a moth to a bright light, I as many were attracted to the cause. I hopped on to the seemingly well-oiled and unstoppable New Labour traction engine steam-rolling along over anything in its path. Badged as the vehicle of change for the common good, the much-quoted stakeholders as passengers on routes and destinations decided behind closed doors.

Many like I became like disciples, following a star in search of a brighter dawn and that elusive rainbow to warm people's souls. For me it led to Downing Street and beyond. In No 10 Tony actually stood on a soapbox amongst the throng and told us that he had all the answers and his charisma flowed hot like molten lava. Who were we to disbelieve the great man with the hair-spray, the tan, the smile and the appeal to the masses. His fine words inspired me and for that reason,

I with many became believers, activists and donors to the just cause for some years to come. Time, effort and money were unwisely invested in the cause, which was to become discredited by unfolding events such as Iraq and the failure to manage MP expenses, never mind applying prudent management to the UK economy. In the early years I and others gave willingly in time and more and many wealthier than me were also to invest in New Labour, generosity and good will. Investment later regretted when political revelations appeared. Damaging revelations and allegations were revealed in the media almost on a monthly basis it seemed. I met the great man Blair on and off his soapbox in various pastoral settings of the political kind, from Downing Street to Coronation Street. He and I as Protestants both married good catholic women of attitude from Liverpool, each to have four children.

A disciple lost, I eventually shed my faith in Tony as a leader of change for the better. After perhaps some soul-searching of a different type some years later Tony went on to change his religion. A new faith, a new start as middle-east peace envoy, plus of course his lucrative fee earning around the world. *Things can only get better* was New Labour's 1997 political anthem and for Tony it probably was true for him when free from the pressures of political office. Many others though are still waiting for that anthem pledge a decade or more on.

I renounced my faith in the party, the Blair/Brown leadership and Government who failed to deliver for the many. Many more have lost that faith and the electorate's opinion of politicians, post 2009 is probably at a historic all time low. Politicians failed because many lacked integrity as role models and just didn't manage the people and the resources well enough. They failed to deliver with the delegated power to which they were entrusted. At Cabinet level in the Blair/Brown government ex-Minister Clare Short on Channel 4 news re the Chilcot enquiry into the Iraq war responded by alleging that the Prime Minister Blair was more interested *in legacy than legality...* she gave the impression that cabinet meetings were more like little chats and that the machinery of government was unsafe. New Labour has had successes under Prime Ministers Blair and Brown subsumed by its many failures.

The Labour legacy leaves the world as a less safe place to live than 1997 with the terrorist, rogue state threat patiently waiting in the wings. In respect of Iraq and Afghanistan on 24th April 1999 at the Economic Club in Chicago Tony Blair made a speech in which he allegedly said: *one state should not feel it has the right to change the political system of another or foment subversion or seize pieces of territory to which it feels it has some claim.* Perhaps when he agreed to send British soldiers off to war he should have reflected on that speech. Especially in Afghanistan where daily news reports about UK soldiers being killed appear with the depressing repetition stating that their families have been informed.

Some people thought that state military intervention and foreign policy had to some degree been formulated against economic benefit and not by appropriate concern for fellow mankind. However the war in Afghanistan appears un-winnable and unconnected to economic benefits. Public services like the NHS have had vast sums spent but not invested wisely over the last decade or so. Parliamentary standards are discredited and MPs as honourable members are held collectively in low repute by the electorate.

The dragon of sleaze has fattened with new heads appearing under the Blair and Brown administration. UK and global environmental/energy challenges have also not been properly addressed by the Government, which raises concerns for the not so distant future. The global credit crunch has exposed the weaknesses in the UK financial systems and has shown that many competitor trading nations are better placed to recover faster.

Labour is no longer a truly democratic party. Since 1997 Labour has lost over 4 million voters and an estimated half of its membership. It suffered five or more by-election defeats as well as the general election. Central control is exerted across the party National Executive Committee, national and local policy forums and the choice of candidates for election. New Labour under Blair and Brown moved past its sell by date lacking adequate finances, lacking sufficient grass roots support and subsequently lost the trust of the people. Pre-General Election 1997 Tony Blair as leader of the Labour Party wrote in his party's *Pocket Guide to policies* that *New Labour were setting out for the general public Labour's agenda for Britain.* He said: *Labour is leading a crusade for change and renewal in Britain.* There it was straight from the horse's mouth I thought, a crusade it was to be and I was signed up as a disciple to the cause. A cause leading to a legacy that most people would describe as of no real positive worth. Tony Blair promised that Labour stands up for the hopes and aspirations of the majority, not just the privileged few.

Deputy Leader John Prescott wrote: *we've had enough of bosses awarding themselves fat pay rises whilst staff have their wages cut.* The pocket guide said *we now have privilege at the top, insecurity for the rest of us.* Events revealed in 2009 show that Prescott's words clearly apply to the Parliamentary members class. He has in 2010 been elevated to the House of Lords, so he will be assured a regular day rate income for attendance. The New Labour legacy of unfulfilled policies and promises over twelve or so years includes not getting their own (Parliamentary) house in order. Events of 2009 showed that the privilege enjoyed by most MPs in the form of salaries, pension benefits and expenses ensured they maintained their position in the top 2% to 3% income bracket across the UK. For the rest of people in the UK, Labour's legacy meant an estimated loss of around £150 billion from pension funds when the dividend tax credit was abolished by Gordon Brown in 1999. Many high profile UK based Labour (and indeed Conservative) Party supporters allegedly still have the benefits of off-shore tax havens with billions out of the reach of the UK authorities. For whatever reason New Labour have failed over a decade or so to address this tax avoidance system.

New Labour promised to reform the health service and opposed a Tory health market, which has created a two tier health service via GP fund-holding and within which Trusts act as competing businesses. They said they would give local people a say in how their health service is run, will make hospitals responsible to the communities they serve. Many NHS Trusts and patient care establishments are run by un-elected Quango Boards who are not accountable to local people.

Although they may invite members of the public to occasional meetings they invariably ignore the democratic wishes of the local majority in such actions as funding for hospices, closure of patient services/withdrawal of life-enhancing drugs on grounds of cost etc. Worthy aims and policies from ongoing political messages, which the majority could relate to came across in that official pocket guide, subsequent manifestos and policy statements. Pledges which attracted me and countless others to the New Labour cause. In terms of Tony Blair not delivering the quoted hopes and aspirations of the majority many, many examples exist. Time was to prove that the fine words were not backed by actions. Failure to respond to overwhelming opposition against the Iraq invasion, failure to respond to public concern of the creeping privatisation of public services - Unison union research found that 9 out of 10 members of the public did not agree with the Government over the use of private firms to run public services.

Another outstanding example of failure to act in the public interest, of blatant hypocrisy whilst the privileged few in Parliament were allowed to abuse the trust invested in them. Whilst some NHS patients were denied essential medication on grounds of cost MPs were allowed to abuse the expense system for years. The democratic majority unaware of how their monies were being milked by the few so called honourable members.

From around 2001 I was a Blair disciple no more. However I was thankful for the memorable experiences with people and events along the yellow brick road of New Labour politics, wondering why the political goal of somewhere over the rainbow was achievable but never reached. A target destination rarely seen under Blair, shrouded by the frequent rain shows of political gloom, grey political intrigue and dark corners of power the sun failed to penetrate. So much could have been achieved with historic political innovation but a positive legacy of the Blair years is sadly lacking substance and compelling evidence of outstanding greatness.

We look back now as, one of the many converts who lost belief in the new dawn politics preached and promised by Tony Blair. A decade of New Labour politics has been lacking in notable achievements with insufficient progress made for the common good. National surveys and public opinion reveal that the nation, as I, are even more cynical and distrustful of politicians. A political cause now bruised and battered, a political legacy lacking in meaningful legacy.

My approach to politics, the search for social justice, my belief in those who promised much drove me, only to suffer great disillusionment because of the many self-serving politicians in high office and positions of public service. When I joined the Labour Party in 1995 I believed in the doctrine *brother's keeper,* preached by John Prescott as well as Tony Blair. I am sure that many, many others in the late 1990s were converted to the New Labour faith by saintly Blair, father Prescott and monk-like Mandleson. I always believed that politics was a process with common good aims by managing resources to make a positive difference in people's lives.

Along the way I experienced the reality that many politicians sadly forget their original principles, purpose and public service responsibilities. The aim of politics is generally undefined and dictionary descriptions detail the process but not the expected outcome or purpose. Political manifestos are useful indicators of short-term purpose but are not tablets of stone and promises made are often broken. My personal goal was to engage in politics as a team member working towards the outcome of a better community and more caring world for us all. Some would say I was too idealistic but I had little time to waste during this lifetime and that was my aim. One of many who wish to change the world for the better.

My role models to bench-mark against our politicians were Martin Luther King, Winston Churchill, William Wilberforce, Nelson Mandela, Lech Walesa and others who demonstrated that one person against the odds could produce outstanding positive change for the good of many. We are all created equal but some of us have a destiny to fulfil if the will is there and the moment is seized. Tony Blair had the potential to step onto the platform of honour with those who made an historical impact for the better in the world. His steps after leaving Downing Street now seem to be already firmly on centre stage for joining the greatly rich of this world. I would describe to others Tony Blair's influence on me as if he took me as a disciple on a long path of hope for bright days and valleys green. A path, which however led to the top of a cold mountain with dark clouds present. I didn't like the outlook on the other side of that peak and his promises made to the many, of which I was one provided no comfort.

The sun set on my New Labour faith and I walked away to valleys new. Hope yet again in my heart for a better political world. Remembering that I told Cherie Blair I would have walked over hot coals to get Tony Blair's party into power I felt like I was now sifting through the ashes. For Cherie though I would perhaps now only offer to hold her designer shoes whilst she walked over those same hot coals for her loved one. I'm sure the effect of the Labour Party machine of spin and manipulation contributed to my disillusionment and leaving of Labour. Being part of the on-message spin machine was just not programmed into my Liverpudlian rooted DNA. Judging by some conversations I had with the Labour Party Head Office androids at Millbank, London, in visits and by phone the androids had indeed landed.

It seemed to me sometimes as if many party employees and hangers on in political circles and New Labour in particular that they had effectively been cloned or programmed on what to say and when to say it. The film invasion of the body snatchers came to my mind where people are being replaced by simulations grown from plantlike pods. Lifeforms who produce perfect duplicates whose only instinct is to survive.

Perhaps they were happy to be recycled cogs in the political wheel being steered and oiled by others. I subsequently left the promised purer than pure Labour Party to promote, with my extremely limited resources political standards, democratic principles and public service values.

During the time I had been in the company of Tony Blair at various events pre 97 and beyond, including No 10 I was very impressed with his oratory skills and the power to enthuse and motivate. Like many others his charisma won me over and I served as a loyal Blair disciple until I saw the light of reality exposing the shallowness of his promises to serve and be totally accountable to the people. His term of office starting with the memorable pledge on *purer than pure* politics that many now misquote as his whiter than white statement. Political standards making, made on the steps of No 10. During his watch as Prime Minister the nation experienced an unprecedented growth of misinformation, spin, the decline of public life standards, the erosion of democratic accountability and political values.

Labour Party so-called policy forums emerged for party members, which turned out to be stage managed talking shops with members' ideas, policy proposals and innovative ideas spirited away into a black hole or shredder. Countless ideas allegedly sent to London with conference motion proposals, but never to see the light of day back at Constituency level. Democratic input shredded effectively by the so called control freaks and political androids. I like many believed that democracy during a decade or so was slowly being chipped away by New Labour and state interference from Whitehall down to local government which was intruding into all our lives. Political correctness gone mad and complete disregard for the will of the people. An erosion by stealth eating away at our liberty, privacy and stifling real participation in decision-making.

A ten-year merry-go-round of sleaze and allegations of concern emerging almost on a monthly basis. Ministerial resignations and failure by the Government to honour the seven principles of public life. Standards embedded in those principles including honesty, integrity and selflessness etc to bench-mark against and to uphold. Standards promoted by New Labour to address sleaze situations arising allegedly during the previous Conservative administration. Those clearly defined standards communicated to MPs but ignored by many as the MP expense scandal unfolded.

As disciple during the reign of Blair I became increasingly disillusioned with unfolding events and I suggested to Cherie that if Mr Blair continued on the same path he would never be considered as a great Prime Minister. Perhaps only considered by some as a good Prime Minister. That now seems to be the case as public opinion and surveys would suggest. That is his legacy. A better Prime Minister than Gordon Brown some would also say, but rarely described as a great Prime Minister by the electorate. Tony Blair and I as many wanted to make the world a better place.

He had a decade of power and great opportunity to wage peace and make a positive difference in this world. I had little power but a powerful spirit and vision to match, or so I thought. Through him I hoped for a better world for the many and not just for the few just as he preached. Hope for the stakeholders in our society, of which stakeholder is now a term of political PR consumed as past its sell by date to the waste-bin of pledges made. Sadly most people believe as Prime Minister that Tony missed a once in a lifetime opportunity.

His legacy as it stands is notably, the Iraq war aftermath, 600,000 or more killed or maimed according to some estimates. Terror emerging in other places, new avenues lined with despair. Countless new tears shed, lives broken, dreams shattered and a cry to heaven by the innocents for relief to their suffering. There is no lasting nostalgia for Tony's impact on the many and statesmen-like achievements originated by him are relatively few over the decade in power.

I did have so much faith as a Blair disciple and hoped that he would truly work for the many rather than the few. To be fair some good things were certainly achieved during Blair's premiership including the Northern Ireland agreement (started by the Conservative Government), the Kosovo/Serbia peace initiative, intervention in Sierra Leone etc. The extra billions pumped into the NHS, education, welfare etc were much needed but badly mismanaged. However it is easy to spend money but it takes skills, knowledge and experience to ensure that money is well invested and achieves the desired people benefits and outcomes. In general terms many senior politicians may have a track record in academic, legal or public sector roles, union work etc. but many often lack the vision, the experience and passion shown by others, like entrepreneurs who have experienced real life challenges and daily decision making, planning and the vital evaluation of the outcomes of policies.

To be fair the strains and stresses of running the country must be immense and to be an armchair critic is easy. However life is too short to miss opportunities, too many other lives depend on not just strong but effective political leadership. Unpopular policies were often presented as tough decisions. The overwhelming majority of those tough decisions never to impact on the privileged, cocooned lives of the MPs. Decisions presented as a macho, brave thing to do even, which attempts to divert negative attention away from the decision maker who will need your votes one day. Aged 43 Blair started his premiership with a clean slate, clean hands and a white shiny smile outside No 10 in May 1997. Hopes were raised and there was for many a feeling of euphoria across the country. All the chosen Labour Party workers called in from many parts of the country waving flags in Downing Street that day they thought, as I did, that they had won the lottery. It is such a shame that the new start saw a ten year political process of ongoing sleaze allegations, cronyism, spinning, reduced standards, gradual erosion of people's rights, intrusion into personal privacy and democratic decline under Blair's Government.

When as Labour Party Leader Tony Blair said *I am my brother's keeper* it now sounds resoundingly hollow along with the other sound-bites, many of which probably originated in the United States political arena. He may have cared for some of his brothers during his journey, but along the way overlooked many other members of the world family in Burma, Darfur and Zimbabwe to name a few.

It is a so sad that after having so much good will shown to him by the British electorate that people struggle to list Blair's successes across the world stage and many believe his legacy is sadly lacking. Iraq is the badge that Tony wears and will always wear unless divine intervention provides global opportunities for him to change the world for the better. His new badge appearing is multi-millionaire via his consultancies, public speaking fees and perhaps further book sales.

Hopefully his and Cherie's charitable foundations will bear fruit one day for the global good. Another potential opportunity for Tony Blair was perhaps a successful role in Europe.

However a European poll by The Times newspaper in 2007 suggested that the majority of those polled did not want to see Tony Blair as First President of the European Union. Perhaps he will make a breakthrough in his role as Middle East Peace Envoy. However in that role, some six months after his appointment it was alleged that he had not yet visited the Gaza Strip, which is like a land-locked country surrounded by high prison walls, barbed wire and filled with despair. A breeding ground for unrest and more.

A nation, collectively guilty and punished because of the few who fire rockets into Israel. A nation under house arrest by the Israelis or so it seems. Although personal security issues are a concern for envoy Blair the Gaza Strip and not five star hotels and palatial conference centres should have been the first place to start in waging peace. The media reported in May 2008 that Tony Blair's much trumpeted Middle East role costs Britain in excess of £400,000 a year. Luxury for some, whilst fellow humans live in abject poverty in Palestine. Hopefully with time envoy Blair may make a difference and forge a legacy recognised by the world. His example as a Christian perhaps forging a different legacy. It is interesting to recall that in 1996 Tony Blair was alleged to have said; *I can't stand politicians who wear God on their sleeves.*

As he prepared to launch his Tony Blair Faith Foundation in New York in May 2008 it was also reported that he had vowed to spend the rest of his life seeking to unite the world's religions A worthy aim but highly doubtful whether some religions would warm to his words considering his failure to intervene positively to save lives in Darfur, his invasion and death creating policy on Iraq, his views on Iran and the tactics in Afghanistan against those resisting the invasion by the infidels.

A decade or more ago I and many others saw him as a force to bring social justice, values and more to this land and beyond these shores. I believed in him as a person, believed in what he promised as a politician. I believed what he preached, delivered with the passion of a great orator who in many ways failed to match the fine words delivered; words spoken with the skills of an Oscar winner in Hollywood. Blair, the movie - blessed are the peacemakers perhaps.

Tony Blair had the potential to step onto the platform of honour with those who made an historical impact for the better in the world. His steps after leaving Downing Street now seem to be already firmly on centre stage for joining the greatly rich of this world. But time will tell whether and how much he and Cherie will invest of the great sums of money earned for their services. Invested perhaps for the greater good through the Blair Foundations for those in need around the world.

The next Prime Minister Brown was chosen for office and yet the allegations against MPs continued in a seamless handover of power and leadership failings. I met Prime Minister Brown the first time at a crucial By-election in 1997 and warned him in a one to one meeting and by correspondence of the wasted millions of public monies on failed NHS computer systems. He ignored the warning signs then. I also met John Prescott briefly and passed on details to his PA about the NHS mismanagement with other information regarding targeted support for small businesses who create the most jobs in the economy. Neither Prescott nor Brown followed up the initiatives. Twelve years later the wasted millions had become £26 billion or more under Labour economic mismanagement across the NHS, Child Support Agency, Passport Agency and Family Credit system etc.

The expression by me years later conveyed to Cherie suggesting the Government couldn't organise a drinks party in a brewery was in my mind must appropriate. She knew of course that I was just being polite and meant that they couldn't organise a piss-up in a brewery. Her reply was not to change my opinion.

The alleged prudent Chancellor probably wasted more monies than any other Chancellor in the history of Parliament as judged by collective ministerial failure to transform public services in line with the sums invested.

The NHS as one classic example of taxpayer billions spent on management consultancies, ineffective computer systems, Quangos etc but resulting in a service that lacked sensible targeted investment. In December 2009 it was announced that large parts of a £12 billion NHS patient record system was to be put on hold as Chancellor Alistair Darling attempted to save public expenditure. The project was said to be £billions over budget whilst patient waiting times rose. Again if this happened in industry or commerce those managing the project would face dismissal and companies would fail. In opposition Labour promised to drastically reduce the number of unaccountable quangos spending tens of billions of taxpayers monies. It never did but it could have achieved that aim. In January 2008 an independent report showed that NHS productivity had fallen over the last decade even though the spending had been unprecedented. NHS data in March 2008 showed that average waiting times for inpatients was 41 days in 1997 but had lengthened to 49 days in 2007 - despite spending doubling to £90 billion in the same period.

Still a service lacking in resources to provide life changing drugs for cancer or dementia sufferers, lacking timely solutions to prevent super-bugs taking lives at ward level etc with posts for newly trained UK Clinicians few and far between. The incidences of the elderly and vulnerable as patients being discharged from hospital malnourished has according to the British Medical Journal almost doubled to 140,000 as estimated in the tenth year of Labour's investment in the NHS. For ailing patient relatives those monies just aren't available for patient care at the point of need. The post-code lottery of patient care is still alive and well under New Labour. Yet out of the Treasury pot of thirty or more £billion is miraculously found to bail out ailing banks. The UK banking bail out and effect on the public purse is yet to unfold and the effect of the eventual downturn in the world economy is a prospect to be faced with these immense sums of public monies already spent or pledged.

Again billions of taxpayer monies are hidden off the public purse balance sheets by Government inspired roll out of PFI schemes. The Private Finance Initiative, which contracts the private sector in public service schemes in the NHS etc effectively produces long-term excess costs to our nation's finances. Long-term debt of billions to be serviced for decades and hidden off the country's balance sheet and spending formulas. A legacy for our families to face when the fall-out of the economic recession hits home and swingeing public service cut backs undoubtedly hit the weakest hard. Failing to preserve, secure and develop strategic energy supplies for our nation will perhaps be another legacy of governmental mismanagement, which will cost billions and create widespread disruption in future years not so far off.

Before New Labour formed a Government they produced a pocket guide outlining all their policies. On the subject of energy the policy stated that: *Britain has substantial energy resources and we do not need extra capacity. Labour does not see any case for building any new nuclear power stations nor extending the use of existing power stations beyond their safe life.* Whatever the pros and cons of nuclear power it was perhaps a strategic policy decision that will come back to wreck havoc on the British way of life. Especially when we are faced with diminishing off-shore energy supplies and facing a Russian stranglehold on gas supplies to Western Europe, where the taps can be turned off anytime as Russian policy dictates.

Perhaps a Government who behind the scenes saw the writing on the wall regarding energy supplies decided to embrace General Gadaffi of Libya as a fellow world statesman. Prime Minister Blair visited Libya in 2007 to kick-start the process of Libyan reintegration into the world community. The fact that Libya had massive oil and untapped gas supplies that could be piped to Europe was perhaps a strategic political consideration. Libya's alleged role in the Lockerbie aeroplane bombing, potential WMD, the alleged support for terrorists etc were now issues of the past. Perhaps a timely diplomatic visit by Tony Blair to meet President Saddam of Iraq would have prevented the Iraq war. New Labour's legacy is effectively Tony Blair's legacy as he was the beating heart of the project and set the scene for policies and Government actions. The General Election in 2010 was a test of that legacy but to many that legacy is a non-legacy.

An inheritance of bankruptcy and unmanageable debt if the nation was a company. Following the demise of the New Labour dream UK citizens have no real nostalgia for the Blair-Brown premierships and will be left to pick up the tab for financial mismanagement over those years. In 2010 the Office for Budget Responsibility forecast that in 2014-2015 the net debt of our nation would hit around £1400 billion leaving

Britain with a larger budget deficit than France, Germany and Japan and even greater than Greece, Italy and Portugal. Greece in 2010 was selling off some of its national assets including some Greek islands to fund the debt crisis. Perhaps the coalition government may start to sell off some of our assets to the rapidly expanding power-house economies of China and India.

The legacy left by New Labour includes annual interest charges on the debt alone estimated at £70 billion by 2015. Some 20% of national growth came from public spending which has been compared with the economy of the old eastern bloc nations. Private sector jobs have fallen by one million under Labour with the state workforce up by over 100,000. On immigration high profile Ed Balls admitted in an interview that Labour had got it wrong and that around 4 million people had entered this country during the Labour years. Their policy he admitted had led to British workers having to accept lower pay and worse working conditions. Labour MP, Andy Burham said that *Labour was in denial over immigration.* That comment brought me back to the point I had made with Cherie Blair about immigration some years back. In March 2006 Tony Blair told Michael Parkinson, the TV presenter, that the decision to engage in the second Gulf War was *made by God as well.*

Of course Tony had forgotten the critical comment he had made some years before in America about politicians *who wear God on their sleeves.* It was reported in the media that Tony also Blair spoke of *God's judgement* regarding the invasion of Iraq. It was also reported that a month before invading Iraq in February 2003 Tony Blair had an audience with Pope John Paul II. The Pope told the Prime Minister that a war would disturb the whole of the Middle East region and exacerbate tensions that are already present. The

Pope was of course right as events turned out and the Prime Minister must live with his decision not to wage peace rather than war with Iraq. At the end of Tony Blair's session of questioning during the Chilcott enquiry into the Iraq war in January 2010 Sir John Chilcot asked Blair *whether he had anything else to add.* Allegedly his reply of *no* was followed by Chilcot asking: *Do you have any regrets, Mr Blair?* Mr Blair replied: *No. No regrets.* Some members of the public audience, which included many bereaved families of service men and women killed in the war could not remain silent any longer. One man stood up and shouted: *Come on, Mr Blair, there must be one regret!* Two bereaved parents of the Iraq conflict allegedly broke down sobbing with another shouting: *Surely, Blair, you regret the death toll?*

Blair allegedly left the room without words of comfort to the bereaved. Some Christians, myself included alongside the majority of the human race, would consider the absence of regret for massive loss of life at odds with our beliefs. With our inherent value for human life most Christians would consider regret and sorrow for such massive loss of life at the forefront of our faith. When former Deputy Prime Minister John Prescott, now Lord Prescott, attended the Iraq war enquiry his opening statement expressed his deepest sympathies to the relatives of the 179 British service personnel killed in Iraq. For that he showed compassion and good sense in contrast to Blair's silence previously at the enquiry regarding regrets or otherwise.

Clearly Blair at this point in time missed the opportunity to express that sentiment of regret for the innocent victims of that war. I am sure he must have felt it inside. Again waging peace by diplomatic means would have been my choice and most people's chosen path to avoid mass death, destruction and pain, which becomes a living legacy of sorrow to those directly affected. To many Blair often came across as a messiah like figure with his crusading ways. Although with time many things did get better for some people. However an outstanding legacy of pride and achievement was never bequeathed to the nation by Blair, Brown and New Labour. Perhaps the New Labour theme song should now be *Yesterday* by the Beatles. Especially the words: *Suddenly I'm not half the man I used to be... there's a shadow hanging over me... I believe in yesterday...* A unique legacy mostly of negatives, a cocktail of mixed elements and outcomes is the legacy of the Blair/Brown New Labour project.

Legacy effects both positive and negative exported around the world touching the lives of many. To be fair our political leaders and politicians are all human, have human frailties and make mistakes as we all do. The problem is that they are elected to serve and not to make mistakes. Mistakes in policy decision making, which can reach out in a ripple effect affecting us all. For some though the wrong policies can result in a life changing tsunami effect by those adversely touched by those policies. Anybody at any level can come up with policies.

But it takes special people with the right skills, knowledge and experience blended with leadership qualities and a strong sense of right and vision to deliver policies of quality with positive outcomes. It takes people of vision and skills who can evaluate and manage that vision to a successful outcome that all can see and benefit from. New labour's legacy still lives on and history will judge the Blair/Brown years. However the outcome of the 2010 coalition government will undoubtedly have a strong bearing on how people reflect on New Labour's years in power. If things go smoothly for the coalition then Labour's legacy will be considered quite negative by many people. If swingeing cuts across public services result in joblessness, hardship and public anger then strikes, street demonstrations, violence even may emerge on our streets. People may then look back to the Blair and Brown years with nostalgia with a wish to see New Labour return, re-badged with a new team to save the world.

13

DEMOCRATIC EXCELLENCE

The United Kingdom with a well established democratic system and stable society has been the political model for many countries and emerging democracies. Millions of disenfranchised and oppressed citizens in the world community of nations look to the UK with hope in their heart for such a system. Our Parliamentary and democratic system, which was once a system to be proud of, has endured disrepute because of failure by political leaders to prevent the abuse of trust and to deliver the just will of the electorate. With all systems evolution is constant and positive and negative forces continually come into play. In the case of Parliament the negative force had been allowed to take hold and flourish for years. Over the last 15 years or so the ongoing events described by the media in headlines of sleaze, political spin, abuse of MPs expenses, political correctness etc have tarnished the English Parliamentary and Governmental system.

The nation in 2009/10 yearned for radical solutions from the political leaders and the political establishment to ensure that democratic excellence is restored and developed even further. Sadly political leaders over that decade and more were shown time and time again to be incapable of exerting their power and implementing effective solutions to gain the trust of the British people. The word democracy originates from the Greek *demos* meaning people and *kratos* meaning power. However people power is still an aspiration rather than a reality for the majority of British voters.

The power of the people is only exercised every four of five years or so at the ballot box. In between elections attempts at people power and public pressure is reflected with petitions, demonstrations, lobbying and letters/emails to MPs and the media etc. Seeking to be part of the decision making process in policies affecting society generally frustrates most citizens. The millions who marched and protested against the Iraq war were proved right and Blair with his Government proved tragically wrong. People power was right then but power to influence was not in the hands of the many. In many ways stakeholder attempts to participate in democracy are met with lip service by politicians.

Proposals or constructive criticism to MPs is like water off a duck's back. For many politician's replies to constituents like *I have noted your comments* or similar patronising comments is the usual brush off. MPs are in power for four or five years or so with all the benefits of the top 3% income bracket of the UK and have total job security and the perks that go with that privileged/protected post. That financial padding and the knowledge that they are not subject to periodic appraisal say on an annual basis like many in the UK workforce places them on a pedestal up and above the rest of society and the people they represent. In talks with political insiders over the years I was appalled to be told that allegedly some MPs did not even hold MP surgeries or meet with constituents seeking MP support.

Much of their work was allegedly passed on to MP assistants and caseworkers who earn a lot less than the representatives of the people. Surveys and public opinion suggests that people strongly believe they have no involvement in decision making affecting their lives. Living in the country that originated the mother of all parliaments with over a thousand years of seeking to establish better human rights, the British people deserve and expect world class standards of representational service from elected members. The development and outcome of high service standards must meet citizen expectations. All that citizens expect is true democratic representation, value for money, compliance with reasonable standards and appropriate evaluation of the political/public service given. In the real world the pursuit of democratic and political excellence is not a journey of rocket science. Reaching the stars is not the goal and the reasonable expectations of the people for public service can be delivered if politicians respond to the democratic consensus.

If the vision is pursued and the will is there democratic excellence is an achievable goal. Recent events and political revelations over the last fifteen years or so have shown that politicians and civil servants have repeatedly failed to provide adequate standards and remedial measures for correcting inappropriate or under-performing political/public service. Perhaps some politicians cannot see the wood for the trees, never mind embracing a vision of new politics leading to a world class standard for democratic excellence. Perhaps too many politicians have vested interests, are just too busy, or feel they cannot lead the way by their own actions. Some politicians however do deliver selfless public service and have high principles, but after swimming against the tide are often subsumed by the weight of the political machinery.

Citizens deserve a political system, a democratic establishment and a public service they can trust. Citizens require a system founded on high standards that deliver agreed aims that are open to public scrutiny. A system that consults with the people, represents the will of the people and works for the common good, not the chosen few. Like many citizens who entrusted power to the few I believed that that trust had to be honoured with high standards of public service. That trust and power vested was weakened by a failed system of discredited standards and accountability. A system designed by the few for the benefit of the few it seemed.

Over the last fifteen years or so those politicians who failed the electorate had yet found time and resources to introduce a virtual avalanche of legislation, state interference, state snooping laws, thousands of new standards across society, quality assurance initiatives, stupid so-called health and safety rules and politically correct constraints on the people. Yet proposals to apply standards for politicians have been invariably opposed by members, who are fiercely protective of their own perks and subsequently lack credibility with the ordinary voter. A radical overhaul of democratic and political systems was clearly overdue after a decade and more of sleaze culminating in the MP expenses scandals of 2009. The way forward has yet to meet the needs and aspirations of the democratic majority of the electorate. As the politicians had failed to meet the needs of people it is now time for solutions to originate from the innovation of the people.

A better democratic model can only work on a foundation of consultation, communication, accountability and electorate focused standards. I believe there is an achievable vision supported by proposals and structures of what the democratic excellence model should be. This model should also form a basis for politicians to be periodically evaluated on. Democratic service excellence from Government, MPs and key public servants can be achieved by adopting practical initiatives reflecting the democratic wishes and standards required by the people. The way forward is for MPs and politicians in general to sign up to and support a citizen originated and focused code of political standards and objectives.

A process should then be in place for independent periodic assessment by the electorate and stakeholders to assess their representatives against that code. More open access to the democratic system in respect of policy formulation and voter participation is readily achievable by the use of the current and developing digital communication media/technology. On-line voting, text message voting, web-based information/opinions and well structured social networking sites for feed-back and evaluation are available to aid democracy and can be developed further.

MPs could also be developed in terms of standards and service delivery in line with voter's aspirations and the continuous professional development (CPD) approach they expect and often legislate for across the public and private sector. It is revealing and to some degree hypocritical that politicians across the political spectrum up to Government level support and promote people development, process improvements and organisational development standards but for their roles do not make use of the underpinning principle of those same standards. With little effort, at minimal cost, the political class could have sought to benchmark themselves as public servants against world-class standards.

The Government promoted Investor In People standard has now been achieved by in excess of 35,000 organisations large and small in both public and private sectors in 50 countries. Almost 3,000 organisations have maintained their Investor in People status for ten years or more. Originating from the recession of the early 1990s, Investors in People was launched to produce a framework, which would help organisations become more effective by developing and harnessing the skills of their people to achieve the organisation's goals. For many organisations this was a transformational experience driving them forward to achieve professional development and success.

It was originally based on four main principles of (1) Commitment to develop people and the organisation, (2) Planning for those aims, (3) Action to deliver the plans and (4) Evaluation of the people and the organisations performance at all levels. This standard would have been a good framework to structure the political/Parliamentary model for democratic excellence. It could have been the basis for ongoing development if established within a citizen focused, yet uncomplicated framework. MPs in particular, their standards of service, value for money and the outcome of their public role could be benchmarked with transparency. As a standard it is not perfect by any means but it could have produced many benefits if applied to public service by politicians.

In 1995 my brother and I actually proposed in a presentation to the Labour Party leadership in London that the Investor In People standard be utilised by The Labour Party. Our idea was that it could be used as a pre-general election development tool for building the team and organisation against a national benchmarked standard. The proposal was swiftly accepted and Labour became the first political party ever to achieve the national standard. Regretfully they did not cascade the principles of the standard to Parliamentarians or across the democratic model.

Seeking to contribute to democratic excellence in my political journey over the years or had seen me working with various political entities and as a floating voter during election times, I often voted for the best candidate rather than the party. I was however criticised by a few critics for changing party allegiances over those years. Some may say it was like changing credit card companies for the best deals. However I felt I had a unique answer to that point of view. As a birth sign virgo with alleged virgoan perfectionist traits I was perhaps looking for the most perfect political and democratic delivery vehicle. But it didn't exist of course. Maybe it was me just being fickle. Why settle for second best in life, love or politics I thought.

I got involved in politics in 1995 and experienced a short-term flirtation with the Conservative Party. But after seeing what they had on offer for the nation I soon jumped ship. At that point in time I considered that they didn't have a clue on national policies such as the NHS and I quickly became disillusioned. My analogy of the band playing music on the Titanic didn't go down well with them and the Tory ship did indeed sink in May 1997. Moving on to New Labour lasted some years until I left the party because of concerns about their political standards, the gradual erosion of democratic safeguards and the control freak regime taking hold. On 26th February1999 I spoke to one senior officer of the Labour Party about my fears for democracy both within the party and for the nation. He asked me to stay with the party, to stick with it. Out of the blue he asked me to stand as an MP. I reiterated my opinion that I could not guarantee to be on message and had independent views, which wouldn't fit in with the party line when demanded.

He told me he personally didn't want more toady MPs, to use his description and said that at a recent Parliamentary Labour Party meeting at Westminster some Labour MPs had allegedly been giving Tony Blair and Gordon Brown a hard time. In his frank words the hard time was given to the leadership for... *fucking things up* is how he described it. That revealing discussion surprised me but did not stop me from leaving the party a year or so later. The Labour Party's unique approach to democratic excellence was demonstrated over the years by various practices, some of which could be described as strange to say the least.

Some attempting to suppress independent opinion and consensus decision-making. One example of subtle central management control on policy was at the Labour Party Conference in September 1999. I reviewed documents supplied to a senior MP with her conference diary arrangement details. A memo confirmed that a meeting of Labour's ruling body - The National Executive Committee - was to be held at conference 7.30 am, 29/9/1999. The memo was from the Party General Secretary and attached was an agenda with agenda point 2 being office recommendations to NEC on resolutions. Backing that up was a document showing details of two trade union resolutions and an emergency resolution with the heading recommended attitudes to contemporary issue composites 4-5 and emergency resolution. For all three resolutions the term office recommendation was used with the accept recommendation made. To me it seemed that the General Secretary was not relying on those NEC members issued with that memo to vote with their conscience after reviewing the pros and cons of the resolutions.

My reading of the document was that they were directed to vote the way they were told. The three resolutions included issues around the Post Office White Paper, The Working Time Directive and Iran. New Labour, new democratic directives from above it seemed to me. I went on to invest more resources into supporting independent candidates or democratic development objectives. This was an invigorating but also frustrating experience as the old party political system was in disrepute and independent strategies generally embraced innovation and a readiness to change for the better. In broad terms independent candidates and small parties are always disadvantaged by limited finances, resource constraints, media opportunities etc. However they do occasionally have windows of opportunity to win seats and try to make a positive difference to our democratic institutions. The outrage and public concern about the 2009 MP expenses scandal was quickly followed with interest from celebrities and non-party citizens in standing as Independents in the expected General Election of 2010. Only time and events will tell if the electorate is ready for a revolution in representational democracy. A new democratic system forged by independents or by a party developing world class standards.

Perhaps the coalition in power 2010 and beyond will eventually provoke a voters' rebellion and with it a new search for consensus politics, which reflect the will of the people. David Cameron and Nick Clegg have major challenges ahead to sort out the economy and Labour's debt legacy. To be fair they are in a lose/lose situation whereas deep cuts in public expenditure are needed and doing nothing is not an option. In February 2007 I decided to test the democratic intentions of the David Cameron led Conservative Party and wrote to him and a Shadow Minister with detailed proposals for a revived democracy.

My analysis suggested that the majority of citizens: (a) feel powerless and alienated in respect of input into decisions that affect their lives, (b) do not trust politicians and believe politicians to be self-serving, (c) feel that robust standards and accountability is imposed on every level of society by politicians but noticeably lacking within the Parliamentary profession, (d) that politicians are only truly accountable to voters every four/five years or so, (e) believe politicians keen to win the vote at election time, promise much - then vote with the party whip when in office and fail to consult with local people they represent, (f) believe that many politicians fail the electorate by failing to demonstrate leadership and (selfless) public service qualities that society can relate to. The document proposed a new approach of consultation, communication and accountability supported by electorate focused standards for politicians. I presented my analysis and recommendations with the Democracy Trust 12 point MP Code of Conduct for consideration. My submission included extracts from the Power Inquiry.

The Power Inquiry was established with support from the Joseph Rowntree Charitable Trust and was a nationwide consultation into reasons why the electoral turn-out at elections was declining and people were losing faith in the political establishment. Its enquiry board consisted of eminent people and was chaired by Life Peer, Dame Helena Kennedy QC. It resulted in many informative conclusions and sensible recommendations. However to the best of my knowledge those recommendations have not been taken up by the political elite. My proposals to David Cameron were presented with a summary highlighting electorate dissatisfaction/disengagement to be addressed and a proposed new approach to politics:

- *Declining turn-out in elections. Voter apathy and disillusionment with politics in general. Majority of electorate feel they only have power or influence at election time: eg Opposition to Iraq, Afghanistan, NHS drugs policy/Hospital service closures etc.*
- *A prevalent view that 'all politicians are the same' (polls suggest that 70% or more of the electorate do not trust politicians.)*

- *The parties appear similar in respect of promises unfulfilled - (Parties want votes not opinions)*
- *Rise of the unaccountable Quango state. Consultation exercises by politicians and Quangos often a lip-service process when the views of the many are ignored by the few.*
- *Decline in Cabinet Government to more presidential and policy unit decision making process. By-passing of Parliament and even Ministers by un-elected decision makers deciding/announcing policies.*
- *Rise of the use of spin, erosion of civil service independence, control over independent voices - as demonstrated by briefing against (eg rubbishing democratic opposition/character assassination).*
- *Rise of influence in trans-national companies and global institutions*
  (and indeed super-power USA) in influencing UK policies.
- *Whistle - blowers ostracised even though protected by Government legislation.*
- *Ongoing allegations of sleaze and inappropriate abuse of public service positions. E.g. self or party interest before public interest.*

(Some above sourced - Power Enquiry)
The key points of my proposal to David Cameron, Leader of the Opposition were also:

To present a strategy seeking to change the face of British politics by injecting enhanced standards, public service values, real democracy and accountability into an outdated political system failing to gain the desired trust or participation of the electorate. The ultimate aim is to develop a (party led) world-class benchmark for democracy and political excellence, which relates to those who matter in politics - the people.

Method: To seek an innovative approach to maximise electorate participation. Achieved by strengthening democratic processes with a new framework encouraging voter participation and promoting enhanced political standards. A framework, which MPs (and MEPs/Councillors etc) are benchmarked against and which voters can relate to.

Strategy: To revitalise politics with an achievable approach, providing the political will is there.
The aim: To achieve a democracy trusted by the people, accountable, by partnership with the people and evaluated by the people.

I suggested that the starting point was to actually define what is the objectives of politics - in a way that all people can relate to. My proposed draft definition was:

Politics is the framework for, the responsibility entrusted to the few, to develop and implement policies, solutions and resources used for the common good, the just needs of mankind and protection of the world we live in.

I proposed that there were three key Unique Selling Points of what is proposed for MPs to sign up to. These were:

(1) A unique voter-friendly (achievable) set of political standards pledged to all in the Constituency. I suggested that party members/the electorate could vote

on the content of the standard and propose enhancements to develop the standards as required.

(2) A Constituency consultation and web or text based electorate ballot prior to MP voting in Parliament on key issues.

(3) A Unique annual appraisal of the MP by the electorate using web or text based voting and establishing public Q & A sessions with the MP.

Over a decade before I had also made a presentation to the Labour Party hierarchy proposing that the party practices what it preaches by mobilising its membership as a resource to work for the community. I decided to seek to encourage the Conservative Party to consider the same proposal for its membership. The proposal was:

Method:
A new approach to engage Conservative party members and supporters in the community working for the common good/whilst implementing party strategy.

Approach:
By implementing a local and national structure/web resource to identify/ recruit/profile local volunteers/party ambassadors, thus demonstrating that new Conservative policy is both dynamic and effective.

Background:
The emerging philosophy from The Conservative Party would appear to be a genuine will to encourage and develop the third sector volunteer/ community sector including not for profit companies, community groups, social enterprises working for the common good and supporting public services.

Proposal:

That the Conservative Party practise what it preaches by setting the national lead in mobilising party members and supporters right across the economic spectrum in pro-active community actions. The mechanism for this would be to establish local, regional and national data-base information held on websites/links and badged as a Party initiative with support resources open to all members of the community.

For example within a local Conservative Association the initial request to build up a public service data bank of local volunteers (existing or new entrants to volunteering) may bring forward say a plumber who could assist a local family in need (2 hours a month pledged*), a decorator who could help paint a youth club (3 hours a month pledged), a Solicitor who could provide pro bono say one hour of legal assistance per month pledged to socially excluded clients etc. The volunteer support could be notionally costed per value of services offered per Ward/Constituency/Region etc and marketed to the local community and media. Eg £x0000 of resource on offer in X Ward or Y Constituency with full PR obtained for this worthy work politically inspired in the community.*

It would be a 'win, win' situation for all participants, volunteers, party ambassadors and beneficiaries. Clearly a organisational plan would be needed to develop this resource and appropriate branding/structures etc. This initiative is workable and can be managed effectively as a long term project subject to funding and resources being made available. A similar model - (non-political) has been used successfully on Merseyside for a decade now with many case studies and successful outcomes even with minimal resources. Details on application.

A Caring Party in Action....................

I received a thank you letter back from a senior Conservative politician - William Hague, *noting the contents of my* letter and a letter from Cameron's office but that was about as far as my proposal went. It was interesting to see some three years later that David Cameron launched the Big Society in the UK, which sought to encourage volunteers from the community to provide services to others less fortunate in the community. Practising what they were preaching was a thought that came into my mind. They had the opportunity as a party to set a benchmark, to develop the national volunteering model I suggested but failed to seize the day as the saying goes. In March 2009 prior to extensive Daily Telegraph exposure of MPs' expenses and resultant national outrage I decided to try again to promote the Democracy Trust proposed Code Of Conduct for MPs. I wrote to the Daily Mail and had the following edited/published as the feature letter:

Dear Editor

Gravy Train Politics No More ?

I was once a New Labour Adviser* and I also provided support to 'Man in the white suit' ex MP - Martin Bell whose integrity I greatly admired. Pre 1997 I was attracted to New Labour by the speeches of Blair and Prescott who both preached with passion the words: 'I am my brother's keeper'. It has occurred to me that this ethos of New Labour only referred to MP expenses for the good of their families? Clearly I misunderstood the *message at the time. I was asked by a senior Labour (national) figure to stand as a Labour MP. That person then had concerns including 'on-message' career MPs. With me he referred to them as 'Toady' MPs. I became more disillusioned with gradual erosion of democratic principles, the growth of state controls and dilution of our freedoms by New Labour. The rise of 'on-message' Labour politicians, who gave in to the 'control freak' ethos of the New Labour Government was evident. The state sponsored growth of political correctness with the wishes of the few in power over-riding the wishes of the many concerned me greatly. Since 1997 political greed, sleaze and self-interest has flourished even more.*

I successfully undertook the MP national selection process but not wishing to 'sell my soul' to become an MP I left the party. In 2001, I and others, after consultation with Martin Bell MP posted a citizen focused Code Of Conduct to all 659 MPs for them to endorse. The One page Code consisted of twelve principles covering restrictions on personal or family financial gain from office, enhanced principles in public life, developing open democracy, human rights, liberty, protecting environment, freedom of information, accountability and evaluation by their constituents and working in an ethical and moral framework. Out of 659 MPs only 26 signed the code. It was interesting that Tony McNulty MP did not endorse it then. Of those MPs who did sign up 19 Labour MPs endorsed the code. They have complied with that code since 2001. Perhaps the readers of the Daily Mail could view the code and decide whether it should be endorsed by their own MPs?

A photographer came to take my photo for the newspaper. He took about 30 pictures of me, which I found surprising and somewhat embarrassing. Unfortunately the newspaper edited out the last sentence of my letter and did not print the code of conduct for reader's opinions. The third of a page headline against my letter was inserted by the Editor as *MPs are mired in sleaze and greed.* Not my words of course but those of the editor. By email I also sent a copy of the published letter and code of conduct to an influential Shadow Minister I had met with from the Conservative Party. I attached the following note:

The electorate/the country is looking for politicians to live in the real world and conduct their lives subject to selfless not selfish standards. Will Cameron, Chris Grayling and colleagues have the drive and courage to take actions commensurate with best commercial/value added practice to reform political standards to meet the needs of all the people? Self-interest is a hollow, short term 'high'. Politics should be about making a positive difference in people's lives that are served. Too many politicians from all the parties put self-interest first. David Cameron may engage with a hung Parliament next election, he may make a good Prime Minister. If he immediately reforms the greed, self-interest and sleaze simmering on for a decade or more in Parliament he will go on to be a great Prime Minister. He has the choice. I believe he is a good man at heart who has faced with dignity, great challenges in life. His mission is and should be for the greater good and not to protect the 'Old boys network' in Parliament. Over to you David...

The reply offered best wishes and an invitation to meet and suggested that after the events of the last few days big changes are on the way anyway. Well those changes are still in the melting pot and we have yet to meet again. Shortly after my attempt to achieve a political shift in political standards the political shit was to hit the media fan and incense the nation. On 8th May 2009 The Daily Telegraph commenced the in-depth analysis of MPs' expenses, which incensed the public, generated massive interest across the nation and around the world. The Prime Minister Gordon Brown and Leader of the Opposition, David Cameron demanded change, promised a new code of conduct for MPs and established yet another committee to review standards for MPs. Fifteen years before, on 25th October 1994, the then Conservative Prime Minister, John Major MP announced the setting up of the Nolan (later - Neill) Committee on Standards in Public Life with the following terms of reference:

To examine current concerns about standards of conduct for all holders of public office, including arrangements relating to financial and commercial activities, and make recommendations as to any changes in present arrangements, which may be required to ensure the highest propriety in public life.

The results of the Nolan/Neill Committee deliberations was the publication of the seven principles of public life standard for politicians and public servants, Quango members etc. However it was a wasted opportunity to also upgrade MP standards with robust checks and balances that are in line with normal workplace standards for UK citizens. The Committee effectively produced a quality benchmark and rules but failed to monitor or provide a substantive mechanism for dealing with breaches of that standard. Both the Conservative and Labour Governments failed to take seriously the foundation for higher standards in public life proposed by the Standards Committee. It was also reported that subsequent Parliamentary Commissioners for Standards who sought to enhance the political system met barriers along the way in challenging the political establishment. The media reported in March 2007 that the Chairman of the Committee on Standards in Public Life, Sir Alistair Graham, allegedly said *the Prime Minister was personally responsible for collapse in public trust on a par with the dying days of the last Conservative Government.* He said the most fundamental thing is that Blair has betrayed himself. He has set such a high bar for people to judge him and he has fallen well below the standards he set for himself. Sir Alistair said that confidence in the morality of those who govern the country was as low as it was ten years ago despite Mr Blair promising in 1997 to be *purer than pure.*

During my role with New Labour I had on a few occasions met the, then General Secretary of the Labour Party, Margaret McDonagh. One Sunday at home I watched BBC Presenter John Humphries - On the record political show interview Margaret McDonagh who said: *No political party should be able to buy an election.* She said that *if the Neill Commission won't clean up politics then New Labour would.....*Words of course said with passion, but the clean-up of politics was still un-addressed years later. The main problem is that MPs have perpetuated a system that exempts them in some way from the rules and regulations imposed on fellow citizens in the rest of society.

The Parliamentary Committee on Standards in Public Life was commissioned to conduct a review following the MPs expenses scandal in 2009 and heard evidence from 50 individuals or organisations with written evidence from 600 people. Regretfully they conducted most of their enquiry from London and did

251

not visit the English regions to directly engage with public forums. On 16 July 2009 Labour MP, Jack Straw said to Sir Christopher Kelly at the enquiry that there *has been a phenomenal increase in the workload of MPs.*

What would spring to mind from most of the electorate if Jack Straw was seeking to justify the cost of providing the MPs salary and office/ staff costs was diddums - *those poor MPs, how they must be suffering...* In 2009 the backbench salary for MPs was £64,766, which is 2.5 times higher than UK average wage. This is within the top 3% of income. If you also include the salaries paid to spouses/members of family, the income into the MP's family circle is substantial. The taxpayer also makes a 27% contribution to MPs' pensions equivalent to an extra £17,486 for each MP giving them an annual salary/pension benefit of £82,252. We must not forget the many, many weeks when MPs are on holiday, which effectively pushes up their daily rates of pay and perks. MPs who lose their seat or stand down or who are censured by the House of Commons for say misconduct also received a substantial resettlement grant.

Following the MP expense and allowance scandal there were 60 published recommendations from the Committee on Standards in Public Life chaired by Sir Christopher Kelly. Although a positive step forward these recommendations will not secure a Parliamentary establishment of democratic and political excellence that the citizens of this country deserve. However in the autumn of 2010 only 30 of the 60 recommendations had been implemented, which speaks for itself. In particular there seems to be no defined penalties or remedial measures proposed if an MP does not act in accordance with the seven principles of public life or uses public funds to support political activities. Sir Christopher's

Committee recommends that MPs should remain free to undertake some paid activity outside Parliament provided it is kept within reasonable limits etc. This would give MPs who are within the top income bracket in the UK the green light to accept paid consultancies and directorships from companies having a vested interest in gaining political contacts/lobbying opportunities and influence in the legislative process.

If an MP has 65,000 constituents to represent, plus the need to keep abreast of local, national and international issues arising within Parliament then he or she would surely not have any free time to effectively moonlight. MPs would argue that their paid work would give them experience and insight into the business world. Yet there are numerous organisations representing UK businesses whom have the expertise, policies and resources to fully brief any MP on issues and business matters. Delivering democratic excellence with high standards of public service should be one of the key objectives in the MP's job description. The problem is that MPs have never had a comprehensive job description. Additionally they have never been subject to genuinely independent and periodic reviews in line with best practice for the rest of society.

The majority of the UK professional work-force have clearly defined job roles and reviews/appraisal. Considering their responsibilities and the taxpayers' monies invested in MPs this lack of defined job role backed by accountability needs addressing. MPs should be accountable to the many rather than the privileged few. MPs seem to have opted out of the service quality initiatives they promote/legislate for on the rest of society. They are effectively funded by the taxpayer to deliver party whip instructions but not electorate consensus on political decisions affecting us all. In 2009 following the MP expense scandal both the Prime

Minister and David Cameron publicly stated that a code of conduct was needed for MPs. That code by either party leader is still awaited in autumn 2011.

The events of that year as exposed by the Daily Telegraph have shown that too many MPs have failed the people. They have lacked the will, the expertise and leadership to keep their own house in order. Most ordinary people are rightly disillusioned with the political establishment and democratic process, which leaves citizens feeling powerless in their own democracy. Politicians and their appointees have failed to deliver democratic excellence and solutions that meet the needs of the electorate. Even after the recommendations of the Committee on Standards in Public Life chaired by Sir Christopher Kelly many issues of accountability, MP compliance and electorate expectations remain unaddressed. MPs' public service performance never faces evaluation by their constituents except at General Election time. MPs legislate for and promote standards with audits and penalties for the rest of society.

However for the MP role, compliance with professional standards, service quality requirements and penalties for breaches of standards have been seriously lacking. This has been clearly demonstrated by the MP expense revelations. Most MPs fully comply with the party whip discipline for political and career reasons but yet are allowed total freedom by the party leadership to ignore their code on the seven principles of public life and have subsequently abused the expense system for selfish gain.

There is a way forward but the initiatives must now come from the people as the political elite have failed the silent and not so silent majority. Democratic renewal should meet the reasonable needs of the people and not play lip service to the insular world of the political establishment. The blueprint for achieving democratic excellence is not based on rocket science or even political science. It is readily achievable if the renewal initiative puts the electorate first and respects their reasonable rights as equal stakeholders in a modern society. The renewal must give citizens a voice, must seek to develop world class politics as a benchmark for the rest of the world and make MPs and public servants more accountable to the people. The key elements of The Democracy Trust proposed democratic blueprint are achievable if the people drive the changes forward and fill the vacuum left by their elected representatives. But like any new initiative it will take money, support and resources to implement.

The icing on a democratic excellence cake would be an academy, university or institute to be established for the development of professional standards for politicians. Without it becoming too bureaucratic the institute could draw up professional standards and personal development for would be and in post politicians in terms of the principles of public life and public service. This could include serving the electorate, induction frameworks into the different job roles that politicians take, ethics, responsibilities, appreciation of electoral law, legal responsibilities, consultation, accountability, evaluation and communication responsibilities etc, etc. The institute could be called the Institute of Political and Democratic Excellence - IPADE. The people of this country have a historic opportunity to take part in an achievable renewal process, which delivers democratic excellence designed by them. The people must lead where the politicians and the establishment have failed.

14

ELECTION BLUES

The 2010 UK general election was historic in many ways with the first televised live debates between the three main party leaders and the election result of a coalition Conservative/Lib Dem government, which sought to accommodate the hung Parliament scenario. The unfortunate remarks made by Prime Minister Brown in the back of his car with his microphone still switched on was uniquely entertaining to the media, although not the woman he described as *bigoted*. Around 4150 candidates across 141 parties contested 650 Parliamentary seats. 341 independents stood with one independent winning a seat as did the green party. The Conservatives took 306 seats, Labour 258 seats with the Liberal Democrats on 57 seats. The election showed that time was not right for the electorate to embrace an emerging political party or to invest their vote in representation by independents.

Some independents if elected would no doubt have brought a breath of fresh air to the corridors of power by delivering higher standards of citizen focussed public service and true democratic representation of the people by the people. I with many others around the country were to discover during the general election that effectively a democratic apartheid was evident in some sections of the media, which placed small political parties and independents standing in the election at an electoral disadvantage. In many cases they were not afforded a fair opportunity to adequately present their case on TV, the radio or newspapers as did the main parties. The exception was if you were a nationally known celebrity standing as independent. Of course if as some years back an independent chose to wear a monkey outfit that was one way to attract media attention.

This actually happened in the mayoral elections at Hartlepool, north east England and the monkey candidate was duly elected by a majority vote. Stuart Drummond, standing as Angus the Monkey, became mayor in 2002 after standing in his monkey costume as a publicity stunt for Hartlepool Football Club. He was originally a call centre worker and cruise ship waiter. Seven years later in 2009 he was re-elected as Mayor for a third term by the people of Hartlepool, where Lord Mandelson used to be an MP. No other directly elected mayor has won a third term in office.

His win in 2009 meant that four of the 11 directly elected mayors outside London were independent, which is quite an achievement. For the other non-monkey candidates the reality is different and true democratic equality is an aspiration and not a reality. This uneven playing field by the media seems to be tolerated by the Government and the establishment in particular who probably have a vested interest in suppressing the voice of independent candidates and small parties. If elected as MPs many credible citizens of the real world outside the Parliamentary enclave/old boys network could effectively sway the balance of power in future hung Parliaments. On the other hand based on my own experience some prospective independents as some party politicians seem to be motivated by ego and other aspirations and in some cases not the desire to give unselfish service.

Some small parties have extreme or perhaps eccentric policies is the perception of many people. But in a democracy they should have the right to fully present their case to the electorate and let them decide.

The media and the BBC in particular - as based on one pre-election scenario explained this inequality away by so-called codes of practise. A prospective independent MP standing in a constituency near Liverpool heard that there was to be a BBC local radio broadcast featuring the main party candidates standing in his constituency. The independent was not invited to be part of the radio broadcast and he subsequently complained to the BBC station organising the event. They replied saying that they had already invited the election panel members and that they had no plans to extend an invitation to him. They provided him with a BBC Code of Practice, which stated that:

Reports or debates about a specific electoral area such as a council ward or a Westminster constituency, should give due weight to candidates of parties, which have demonstrated substantial electoral support in that area... Constituency/ward reports or debates should also include some participation from candidates representing any other parties or independents with either previous substantial electoral support, or with evidence of substantial current support in that constituency/ward.

On the face of it the BBC policy was saying that to gain an invitation to be part of a pre-election candidate programme the candidate had to show evidence of substantial electoral support. A reasonable interpretation of the code would suggest that any citizen who for the first time decided to stand as an independent or as candidate within a small party would automatically be excluded from a BBC radio or TV debate because they were new to the political world and could not prove substantial support before the election day. It was a classic chicken and egg situation whereas access to media, which could positively influence voting intentions was being denied and disregarded citizen rights and equal opportunities principles.

I spoke to ex MP BBC world reporter Martin Bell about the BBC policy and he said there was nothing anybody could do about it and it would be a waste of time challenging the BBC. Reading between the lines it was probably policy to prevent extreme smaller parties from getting air-time. In the case of the highly credible, articulate candidate from Merseyside he had a good track record of local community and local political input but yet allegedly was denied a level playing field platform with the mainstream candidates. What had evolved historically it seemed was a media focus on the three main parties, which prevented credible prospective independent MPs or small political parties from achieving true democratic equality in terms of media coverage.

This was not an exaggeration but a reality based on feedback from prospective MPs and smaller parties such as UKIP, Plaid Cymru and the Scottish Nationalists. In the national TV debates with the three main party leaders a fourth person for example could have presented the case for independent politics and small parties to the nation. This would truly have been equality of opportunities in a world-class political system. However a Government and media, which often promoted equality of opportunity and an establishment, (including the Equalities Commission) did not practise what it preached. I also spoke to Liberty the campaigning organisation twice after sending them an email outlining the issue but they did not have the courtesy to get back to me. Liberty who seek to protect civil liberties and promote human rights. They also quote on their web-site: *article 14 of the Human Rights Act prohibits discrimination in the exercise of a person's human rights on grounds including sex, race, colour, language, religion, political or other opinion, national or social origin, association with a national minority, property, birth or other status. We can only strive for and hope that in future elections true equality in media access that is sensible and practical is developed for those citizens who wish to participate and re-vitalise our democratic system. This fault line in our democratic system must be highlighted and corrected by those who value true democracy as it should be.*

I found it was interesting that in Italy it was reported May 2010, that Italy's top TV newsreader anchor Maria Luisa Busi who presented the flagship TGI evening news quit after complaining that news coverage was biased in favour of media mogul and Prime Minister Silvio Belusconi. TGI was fined by Italy's broadcasting watchdog Agcom for under-reporting the opposition democratic party in favour of Belusconi's party before the March regional elections. So it seemed that Italy had its own problems with alleged unequal media opportunities. The Italian newsreader who quit certainly had professional integrity and is to be admired.

Some weeks before the general election, by email I had contacted the BBC Andrew Marr Politics Show. I politely suggested that every week he wheeled out high profile politicians and celebrities and that perhaps the ordinary man/woman who experience the reality of political policy in the community and workplace should have a voice on the show. My request disappeared into cyberspace. However due to contacts I had made over the years I was presented with a bit of air-time elsewhere. I was invited by a Midlands BBC radio station and a north-west (independent) city radio station to present my views on democratic renewal in the run up to the election. That was an interesting experience and I followed with a short web cam speech on the BBC web-site replying to a question asked of the many UK interviewees on what they would do if in the post of Prime Minister.

A short film in a city centre shopping mall, which only allowed a few statements, delivered nervously as the passing shoppers walked by. Prior to the general election and eventual formation of the coalition government I was to meet some more of the great and the good and other mere mortals, connected with, or aspiring to be elected to political office. They included various prospective independent MPs including wannabe MP Esther Rantzen (based on my contact with her I was not impressed) and other independents from around the country. Future Coalition Cabinet members George Osborne MP and Iain Duncan Smith MP became additions to my expanding political picture gallery. This gallery was supplemented by Labour prospective Stephen Twigg who was some weeks later elected as MP for West Derby, Liverpool. I acquired a sweet photograph of me and Stephen who seemed a really nice guy. He was standing alongside me and appeared to be presenting me with a bunch of flowers. The bouquet actually belonged to Cherie Blair who was also present.

Some months earlier I met the now newly elected Labour MP for Walton in Liverpool, Steve Rotherham. He was to impress me with his apparent integrity and public service values. During various meetings we had a heart to heart on some personal and political matters. He came across as a man of substance with his heart in the right place. I believe as a man of the people MP he will be a great asset to Parliament in future years. Based on his track record as Mayor of Liverpool during capital of culture year, his great sense of humour, political nouse and competencies he will, I believe, do well in Westminster. Steve as Lord Mayor had met the Queen in Liverpool and had joked with her as Liverpudlians do naturally, to which she responded well. Steve told me that she had commented on how young he was to take on the role of Mayor of Liverpool. He responded that she was also very young aged 26 to take on the role as Queen of England when she did. She took it in good humour but Steve said the other great and good dignitaries sitting around the dinner table nearly choked on their drinks as to his direct approach.

One thing he did point out to her Majesty was as people called her *mam* that it was long standing custom and practise by the Liverpool community for sons and daughters to call their mother *mam*. She was according to Steve absolutely amazed and completely unaware of that fact. As a bricklayer/tradesman in his working career and worldly-wise person that he is Steve is just what Parliament needs. Hopefully he can seek to counter the disproportionate balance of public school, millionaire MPs and others who have not lived in the real world as the majority of our electorate do.

Some months before I with others had lunch with Iain Duncan Smith MP who was to become Work and Pensions Secretary in the new coalition cabinet. He was I thought a very sincere man who seemed to have a compassionate insight into poverty and support programmes. His role in cost reduction in saving taxpayer monies across the benefits system should be interesting. Me like the proverbial bad penny turning up I also had a close encounter at a pre-election dinner with Cherie Blair. Fate it seemed put us together in the same room again. My wife was there to keep an eye on me and Cherie weighed Karen up when we had our photograph taken with the *bolshie* scouser Cherie (bolshie was Tony Blair's description of his wife). Of course Tony was not in attendance.

He was probably away saving the world as usual and enhancing his bank account to pay for the modest life-style and five homes or so that they enjoyed. Cherie it seemed was on the election trail that night and in her speech told the gathered admirers that she was supporting around 30 charities and patron of many. She informed us that she was very excited about working on the aborigine case and proud of a case and achievements concerning damages sought regarding children with special needs. Hiding her light under her bushel in the biblical sense did not come across that night. She also reminded us that her father had *abandoned her* when she was eight years old and her mother had to work in a fish and chip shop. Gosh how awful I thought.

The poor thing being kissed each night by her mum who was fragrant with the smell of lard, salt and vinegar acquired in that Liverpool chippy. She did of course work for a living in the local community as many millions of other working class people did and that should have been a positive aspect in her family background and future roles. The media alleged that Cherie was at that event to promote the candidature of a young and attractive prospective Liverpool Labour MP who was allegedly a close friend of her son Euan Blair. Cherie also reminded us that night that she had met two Popes and that it was extraordinary that a girl from Waterloo, Liverpool could end up living in No 10 Downing Street.

She said she now missed the people working in No 10 - all 250 of them. As a Liverpudlian she informed us again that her husband Tony Blair referred to her as a bolshie scouser and that when they were in China he reminded their hosts that Cherie was from

Liverpool. This led to her rendition of the Beatles love song *when I'am sixty four* to the Chinese and world's media.

She said that she certainly had her own opinions on policy and politics but at the end of the day she could not second-guess Tony or tell him what to do. As a gruelling 24/7 job being Prime Minister the last thing Tony wanted was lectures from a bolshie scouser. When asked about critical press reports she said that they could not say anymore than they already had about her. The Daily Mail was mentioned in particular. On the subject of democracy she said that it was a very special thing and that she 100% supports her children going into Parliament.

She went on to say/joke that when Tony was first elected in 1997 and she was caught out by the photographers opening her front door in night wear with unmade hair that she was setting the trend from Liverpool. She told us that ex-President George Bush had a good sense of humour and the first time they met at Chequers she bent his ear about the United States death penalty. Also she said that Bush had apparently said to Tony Blair *l will say it in Texan Tony - you say it in English*. She revealed that when they met at Crawford, USA with Bush she had another discussion with Bush and as he left the room he had to ask Condeleza Rice what was the treaty that they had just been discussing.

Following a question about Tony Blair appearing in the Chilcot enquiry into the Iraq war she said that not a day goes by that Tony does not think about him sending the troops into Iraq. However she said he was proud of his military intervention into Sierra Leone and Albania to prevent bloodshed between the warring factions and offer protection to innocent civilians.

I wondered after hearing that particular statement was Cherie aware that in the Sierra Leone conflict that the British armed forces who went in ostensibly to protect British nationals was led by a resolute British army commander of independent mind who framed the policy of intervention there. The commander had unilaterally decided to go on the offensive and stop the rebel insurgents killing and maiming innocent people. The rebels had demonstrated their brutality by cutting off the arms of their opponents, including mainly innocent civilians. Apparently for some weeks the British commander had for humanitarian reasons decided to wage war on the rebels whilst back home in Whitehall the civil servants and politicians discussed and agonised about the intervention option and issues.

Finally the Government led by Tony Blair backed the successful military campaign initiative, which was already underway. Cherie said that as a result of Tony Blair's various military interventions that many boys at birth were given the name Tony by the grateful people. Perhaps the name of the heroic soldiers leading the campaign to protect the innocents would have been more fitting as a role model tribute to their courage in the killing fields.

At another political event Labour MP Andrew Miller, for Ellesmere Port and Neston, was to amaze me with his frankness, but in my mind lack of sensitivity about people's opinions following the MP expense scandal. He told the audience in his pre-election hustings meeting that he had just started to enjoy the Department of Work and Pensions winter fuel allowance now paid to him. Clearly the full package of £100,000 or more in MP salary/ expenses etc to support his considerable income as an MP was lacking somewhere. Perhaps he had the heat turned down at home before he got his winter fuel allowance. I wondered if he ever supported legislation for applying means testing to the benefits system. However he was voted back into office by the local electorate who were no doubt oblivious to his winter fuel allowance, which he clearly didn't need based on his MP salary and expense allowances. Perhaps his very rich MP colleagues, especially the millionaires, should have their income means tested before MP expenses and benefits are awarded. Practise what they preach perhaps?

Would be Independent MP, TV celebrity Esther Rantzen was certainly a memorable character based on initial impressions. In my case she came across as sadly lacking in tact and diplomacy during my contact with her. Based on my own personal experiences during meetings/talks with her she consistently failed to impress me. In my opinion she had succeeded in alienating me who was trying to help her. I was with ex MP Martin Bell and others who were asked to present campaigning techniques to a meeting of around 50 would be prospective Independent MPs prior to the general election in May 2010. At the onset of my presentation I made it quite clear that there would be a Q & A opportunity at the end of the session.

I suggested that those with previous campaigning experience who had stood before in elections do bear with me. Especially if there was overlaps of campaigning advice from previous speakers etc. Five minutes into my talk Esther interrupted and said to me and the audience that *we know all this*. She asked *had the campaigning strategy ever been evaluated*. I assured her that it had been used/evaluated for a highly successful constituency by-election victory, taken as a model of good practice for Labour's North West key seats campaign. It was also structured on the successful Martin Bell election campaign victory in 1997 and developed since then. She took it upon herself to speak for all in the room, the majority whom she had never met before. Her interruption annoyed me and many others in the room, the majority who had never had the experience as prospective MPs running campaigns.

Many delegates came up to me afterwards to express their dismay at her interruption as self-appointed spokesperson for the 50 or so assembled. Experienced campaigners did offer thanks to me on some presentation points/ideas taken on board. They shared their various opinions on Esther. One actually described her as *Esther rants-on*, which he thought amusing. She was also rude to my wife in abruptly telling her that she was standing by seats, which Esther wanted to reserve for the second half of the seminar. Esther's seating was actually table-tops at the back of the room where my wife was sorting my presentation hand-outs on.

Previous to that I was sitting next to Esther and her entourage on those tables and tried some Liverpool humour on her. She was next to me discussing whether to have her photograph taken with some of the other prospective independents. She declined as she did not want to be seen to be endorsing people she had no knowledge of. That was fair comment I thought. But I said to her jokingly, how about getting your photograph taken with me Esther - *as a tall, darkish and once allegedly good looking scouser, that would add surely value to your campaign?* Esther looked down her nose at me as if I was dirt on her shoe and failed to respond. Her sense of humour probably having a day off. That's life I suppose. She should in my opinion have stayed in the jungle in Australia as in *I'm a celebrity* - keep me in here - with the creepy crawlies for supper.

When I spoke to Esther at our first meeting some months before I asked her to endorse the Democracy Trust code of conduct for MPs. She said she couldn't possibly endorse it *as she would have to continue working at her media jobs if elected as MP*. I politely asked her again by email months later to endorse the code of conduct, which would have meant her only having one paid job as MP. That email was ignored/not replied to. During her campaign and no doubt linked to her celebrity status and media contacts Esther had various articles printed notably in the Daily Mail, which was very helpful to her. Helpful to her but not to the local highly credible and principled independent candidate.

His name was Joe Hall who was not afforded equal opportunity to present his profile nationally. However she failed to win the constituency seat on election-day but managed to persuade with her warm smile, sense of humour and innovative manifesto around 1800 Luton citizens to vote for her. It was reported that sometime after the election that the newly elected Labour MP she stood against invited her for lunch. However I was very mindful that she was instrumental in establishing the national charity *child-line* some years before and she deserves full credit for that fantastic service that has helped tens of thousands of children.

During the general election campaign I met George Osborne MP, then Shadow Chancellor, and reflected with him on stage nerves during his hustings meeting. I had my photograph taken with him by an exit door with the exit sign showing clearly above our heads. I wondered whether one day that photograph would ever be used by the Private Eye magazine at some point when George encountered a change of fortunes in political circles. I and the constituency audience listened to his stated greatest achievement during his 9 years as MP. He had said that as MP for Martin Bell's old parliamentary seat - Tatton, that *obtaining a cochlear ear implant for a young boy in his constituency was his greatest achievement*.

Noble as the cause, the satisfying outcome for the boy and his family I thought of other overarching objectives and worthy causes for the common good he could perhaps have also focussed/reported on. I reminded him that I had chaired his original hustings meeting many years before when he was elected MP. The hustings that night in 2010 had pre-prepared questions from named local constituents addressed to each candidate. Questions like why Starbucks cafe had closed down in Knutsford town, the future of Knutsford medical centre, the planned phasing out of cheques by the banking sector etc.

There were no questions on the economy and dealing with the national debt for the future Chancellor of the Exchequer, which I found very surprising. One candidate that night however was very entertaining. He was standing as the *True English Poetry Party*. He was a scream and brightened up the night with his responses to questions, some of which he replied that he didn't have any opinion. The panel of candidates were asked about their own moral compass. The poet replied that he had some flaws, but said *he was a poetician and not a politician*. He actually said to the audience that *I am not looking for your vote*, which caused great amusement with the panel and the local constituents. In response to the audience at one point he replied that *I have nothing useful to add on this question.*

Some in the audience thought he would, on the basis of his presentation make an interesting addition to the back benches of Parliament. Just under 300 people did eventually vote for the poet at the subsequent election. George Osborne responded to the moral compass question by saying that he would do to others as you do to yourself......*but I'm only human. In politics you get all sorts of things flung at you.... people must judge me on my merits*. Sarah Flannery, the independent candidate reflected on the MP expenses scandal and said that *the main principles of justice, honesty and integrity were her beliefs, which directed her own moral compass.*

The Labour Party contender put forward his belief in community and told the audience of his role as trustee for the £25 million turnover MIND charity. He was very honest with the audience and told them about his own challenges of illness, which he had overcome and said that it had added insight and experience into his charitable work. Out of two general election hustings I attended in 2010, one Tory, one Labour it was noticeable that all the questions debated in the public meetings were submitted beforehand and that there was no time allowed for questions from the local constituents on the night. This to me was disappointing and did not encourage open democracy, straight talking nor did it allow constituents the opportunity to hold their standing MPs to account. Standing against George Osborne in the general election was community activist and talented business lady, Sarah Flannery who as an independent was seeking a better type of democracy of the people. A few weeks before the election I got an email from Sarah saying that Martin Bell had given her my contact details.

She said that Martin had described me as one of the *wizards* of his 1997 campaign and said *I should speak to you*! Well that is the first and probably the last time I will ever be described as a *wizard*. I met with Sarah and colleagues one lunchtime in Knutsford and gave Sarah what advice I could, with some limited assistance by telephone and email as well as attending her public meeting husting with George Osborne and the other candidates. She drew a respectable 2243 votes in the constituency which compared to many independents was an achievement considering her short campaign opportunity. The 2010 General Election result was unique in recent UK political history. A resultant rainbow coalition Government formed out of political necessity with Conservatives and Liberal Democrats forming what some would call an unholy alliance of political bed-fellows. Some sleeping head to toe and some in the future to be head to head on issues and policy differences perhaps.

Mocked by some as the Con-Dem alliance the two party leaders of David Cameron and Nick Clegg now smiling side by side like a church wedding with both, for the time being singing from the same political hymn sheet. The last coalition had happened in the UK during the second world war in 1939 and perhaps the challenges of the economic state the UK was in was similar to a war like footing. Especially considering the unprecedented national debt and future pain the nation was facing. Only time will tell whether David Cameron as the third (then future) Prime Minister I have met will become a great Prime Minister. Perhaps third time lucky in my case.

If real people from ordinary backgrounds are brought into his policy making then he stands a good chance. If the ex lobbyists/public school stereotypes provide the advice and policy then things may go pear shaped, the coalition may fall apart and David Cameron's legacy will be lost in the swirling waters of political history.

15

DEMOCRATIC BLUEPRINT

The blueprint for a revived democracy is indeed not rocket science but quite simply a structure to meet the just needs of the people. It is based on elected representatives signing up to a citizen focussed set of public service standards with the MPs being appraised by constituents on an annual or periodic basis. The other key element of the blueprint is that the MP is not dictated to by a party whip on how to vote in Parliament. The constituency MP follows policies and voting intent in line with constituent's consensus in true democratic representation. The use of digital democracy, website/text voting has an important role to play in this process.

Democratic and political excellence should be driven from the top by innovative leadership, vision and integrity. Leaders actually leading by example and inspiring others to follow on shared common good aims are an important element in a just society. One such leader with around fifty years' service as a politician, Sir Winston Churchill often reflected on his Parliamentary experiences.

He wrote: *Party politics are necessary if a focused opinion is to be brought on public life. Party has a place in a nation, but people must see to it that the nation is not subordinated to the party... The tendency of political parties to discourage individual thought and independent views may suggest one reason for... the fact that Parliament has declined in public repute*...* Half a century and more later the opinion reached by Sir Winston still holds true in contemporary politics. He was a visionary, a great Prime Minister, a statesman who although having faults, as we all have, brought inspiration to many millions both home and abroad during the war years.

*Compilation in book - 'I lived my life again' by Jack Fishman, published by W.H.Allen in 1974.

On the subject of great Prime Ministers as I pointed out to Cherie Blair in February 2004 that; *Tony Blair the PM may leave office considered as a good PM but, if things don't change, he will miss that wonderful opportunity to be considered as a great PM.* Sadly that still seems to be the case even in 2011 with most people critical of Tony Blair's term of office, his lost opportunities as Prime Minister, leader of the nation and more recently – middle east peace broker. In Davos in 2006 Tony Blair was reported to have said that this was his last speech there as Prime Minister and that he was looking forward to coming back in the future and telling other leaders were they went wrong. Maybe Tony Blair had seen the film *Back to the Future* and that had given him inspiration to make that statement. Perhaps his own experiences would make him qualified to do the time travel thing.

Prime Minister Gordon Brown effectively took to the Scottish hills after losing the 2010 General Election and kept a low profile. I and many others guessed he was writing a book on his political experiences. The jury of public opinion is still out on performance and achievement levels during Gordon Brown's time as Chancellor and Prime Minister. What is abundantly clear is the scale of the public sector budget deficit, reported as twice as large as USA and Japan. He as Chancellor and Prime Minister left behind that crippling debt for the Lib- Dem/Conservative coalition government to address. Also the pain and misery for millions of ordinary people who will pay the price in lost jobs/income because of previous mismanagement of public monies. The so-called Prudent Chancellor, later PM did not impress me when he failed to act on sensible proposals to prevent wasted £millions (becoming £billions) on public services over the last decade or so.

Yet again I suppose my assessment May 2006 to Cherie Blair that the Labour Government could not organise a drinks party in a brewery was quite appropriate based on what state public finances were in 2010 and beyond. I suppose that most ordinary people think that the great and the good elected to run and serve our country have the skills, knowledge and experience to run a nation and to a degree have taken that ability for granted. The reality is that recent history has shown that many political figures and indeed senior civil servants just do not have what it takes to deliver value for money management of public services and our economy. The skills make up of the coalition cabinet in 2010 more reflects the wealthy, public school privileged few of our society rather than drawing in a cross-section of life experiences that truly reflect our society and its representation.

Parliament and party managed democracy is still suffering public disrepute following the 2009 MP expense and allowance scandal. Party officials often parachute nationally favoured candidates into constituencies as a fait-accompli against the wishes of local activists and local candidates. Sometimes imposed as fresh blood prospective MPs favoured by central command rather than local choice, which surely intrudes into constituency democracy. Effectively a closed-shop approach. Media insight and ongoing revelations reveal the advantages taken by some honourable members and the thread of arrogance and opportunism embedded in some Parliamentarians. Some MPs and Lords in 2010/11 faced legal retribution when the allegations made against them were proven. Independent investigations and reviews are periodically implemented by Parliament but by the nature of the selection process are not independent as say a court jury would be.

Following the public outcry about MP abuses of position in November 2009 the Committee on Standards in Public Life chaired by Sir Christopher Kelly made sixty recommendations on MPs' expenses and allowances. The committee is by custom and practice sponsored by the Cabinet Office with the Chair and members appointed by the Prime Minister. In July 2010 I sent by email a request to the administration team of that committee seeking confirmation as to which of the sixty recommendations had been implemented by Parliament. They could not provide that information to me some nine months or so after the Kelly submission to Parliament.

In response to my email I received a reply from the Parliamentary standards team, which on the face of it was an internal email (8/7/2010) not intended for me. It said: *I suggest you indicate that we intend to publish our annual report very shortly which will include a stock-take on this issue...* I waited for the annual report to be published, which did indeed produce a status analysis of those 60 Kelly recommendations. However some of the terminology in the status column of the report as to whether individual recommendations were implemented or otherwise was to me not very informative. Quite often the status was given as: *the constitutional and governance act 2010 has given effect to this recommendation...* whatever that meant in plain English terms. A simple summary of implemented, not accepted, under review, legislation required etc would have been more meaningful to ordinary people. Hopefully a reader friendly analysis and regular updates of progress made on the recommendations will follow. If this does not happen then progress towards democratic excellence will suffer.

Although a positive step forward the sixty recommendations did not go far enough anyway to develop a Parliamentary establishment of democratic and political excellence that the citizens of this country deserve. In particular there seemed to be no defined penalties or remedial measures if an MP did not act in accordance with the seven principles of public life or for example used public funds to support political activities. Strict penalties were recommended but no attempt was made to equate the penalties to the breach of trust. In the real world of ordinary citizens if people got on a train without a ticket, if they dropped litter, if they exceeded the speed limit or fiddled their tax returns people are fully aware that penalties could or would be applied. In respect of MPs using public funds to support political activities I had personal knowledge of ex north-west MP whose office used Parliamentary letterheads, envelopes and 1st class postage to send a mail out to Labour party members in an adjoining constituency with a Lib-dem MP in office.

The two page letter included an invitation to a £25 per head Labour Party fund-raising dinner with the MP as guest speaker. Some time later there was a newspaper article about the MP being one of the highest claimants of MP expenses – spending nearly £25,000 on postal costs. The MP told the reporter: *It proves we have been the best at communicating with our constituents*. In the article there was a sweet photograph of the MP sitting alongside Cherie Blair with Cherie in a bar or club displaying a rather cheeky smile and drinking a glass of green liquid - perhaps a double lime juice. Seriously though the political mail out was an abuse of taxpayers money and it was allowed to happen because of lax controls or appropriate penalties.

A year or so before Kelly's recommendations the Democracy Trust (and others) proposed as one element of democratic renewal that MPs should face a recall via a by-election if they were deemed to have lost the trust of their constituents. It now seems that the recall option has been taken up by Parliament but only in severely extreme cases. So if any MP was deemed by constituents to be ineffectual or not active in his/her own constituency or side tracked with self-enriching jobs or consultancies then the MP would still be secure for the life of that Parliament.

Sir Christopher's Committee recommended that MPs should remain free to undertake some paid activity outside Parliament provided it is kept within reasonable limits etc. This gives MPs who are within the top 3% income bracket in the UK the green light to accept paid consultancies and directorships. Additional income streams and benefits perhaps from grateful companies having a vested interest in developing political support for commercial gain. An MP has 60000 constituents or so to represent, plus the need to keep abreast of local, national and international issues arising both within and outside Parliament.

Most of the electorate would surely argue MPs would not have any free time to effectively moonlight. MPs often argue that their paid work would give them additional experience and insight into the business world. Yet there are numerous organisations representing UK businesses, the not for profit sector etc who have the expertise, policies and resources to fully brief any MP on social issues and business matters. Kelly's recommendations suggested that *other employment can bring valuable experience to the House of Commons and the income from it can help to preserve independence from the whips...*

On reading that I was amazed to read such rubbish when a MPs income stream has never and will never play a part in deciding whether to vote against the wishes of the party whip. Delivering democratic excellence with high standards of public service should be written into the MP job description. However one problem is that MPs have never really had a detailed job description. Additionally they have never been subject to genuinely independent and periodic reviews in line with best practice for the rest of society.

The majority of the UK professional work-force have clearly defined job roles and periodic reviews/appraisals. Considering their responsibilities and taxpayer's monies invested in MPs this lack of defined job role without periodic accountability to the electorate needs addressing. MPs should be accountable to the many in society rather than to the privileged few like party whips and MP appointed bodies of self-regulation. The police are effectively policing the police is the scenario in place. Time and time again we see so-called independent nominees, committees and individuals selected from the old boy's establishment network, which does not inspire public confidence. Independent champions of standards, public scrutiny and openness have often been marginalized, dismissed or rubbished by the parliamentary establishment who sought to preserve their enclave of power and self-interest.

Many MPs seemed to have opted out of the national and international service standards, quality initiatives they promoted/legislated for on the rest of society. In essence they are effectively funded by the taxpayer to deliver party whip instructions, whipped to vote the party line rather than referring to electorate consensus on political decisions affecting 60 million people here and millions more overseas. The time for change is now and a democratic blueprint (Consensus Democracy) for the people is presented below as a basis for renewal to our democratic and political systems.

The blueprint is not perfect, is open to change, development and restructuring. However it is hoped that some of the components within the structure proposed will in time develop within the UK. Those who seek a democracy of the people, for the people must work together for the common good delivered by ethical politics and democracy as it should be:

Consensus Democracy Blueprint:

It is our belief that any political and democratic system should be based on shared values, high standards of service, accountability and full citizen participation. Politics as the driver of democracy, should strive for common good aims, rights and humanity in the country served and across the rest of the world that we share. The blueprint is designed to introduce innovative universal political standards and citizen focussed structures, which seek to involve citizens more in democracy, political policies and standards in public service. The aim is to make a positive difference in systems that have failed the people and to seek to deliver citizens their full rights as shareholders in society. Shareholders in democracy who can expect high service standards and rightly hold their elected representatives to account on a periodic basis. The blueprint is flexible, subject to development and can be adopted by any political party or independent in the interest of practising true democracy.

This initiative must seek to restore the English Parliament as the Mother of all Parliaments as a model and centre of political excellence to the rest of the world. The blueprint presented is a framework for all people to build on, to reconstruct or to use as a springboard for the future development of a democratic and political system. A system that all can relate to and be content with. To complain and criticise our current system is easy, to design a better way forward and contribute to that evolution for the common good is a greater challenge. A challenge for all those who care about the life we and others live in this world. The negative fall-out from the Parliamentary expense and allowances scandal must now be turned into a positive force to deliver a democratic and political system that all citizens can relate to and can be proud of.

Consensus Key Aim:

To present an alternative political and democratic model to the UK electorate based on democracy as it should be - for the people and reflecting the will of the people.

Consensus Key Principles:

- Aims and desired outcome of politics defined.
- Model/blueprint designed to reform and regenerate politics whilst building up the trust of the electorate, which has diminished over the last decade or so.
- No party whip or political career pressures to suppress/divert focus away from elected

member truly representing the just will of the people.

- Can be adopted by elected/prospective members within political parties, networks or by independents serving their community.
- Unique electorate focused pledges/code signed by the politician, which puts the needs of citizen and community first.
- The Code/standards when endorsed seeks to build electorate confidence in the serving or prospective politician and could positively influence electorate voting intention.
- In conjunction with existing democratic networks and pressure groups to provide resources and support to those wishing to selflessly serve their communities by elected office.
- Consensus would not be a membership organisation but a resource founded on standards of public service endorsed by its stakeholders.
- National/world class standard proposed, which if rolled out could form a benchmark/be utilised by elected/prospective members in all levels of UK, European or overseas Governments.

Short Term Aims:
Elected or prospective politicians to consider being founding stakeholders in Consensus initiative and co-sponsor of political renewal across the country.

Medium Term Aim:
To roll out principles/build up stakeholder base across rest of country by media awareness/promotion with other democratic stakeholders.

Longer Term Aim:
Consensus resources/infrastructure established and democratic models developed/promoted to existing and emerging democracies globally.

Consensus Organisation:
To establish a democratic network/'think tank', resource and support facility with web-site/help-line service to promote democratic and political development based on high standards of public service, which is citizen focussed rather than party driven.

Consensus aims:
To develop the principle that any political and democratic system should be based on consensus, shared values, high standards of service, accountability and full citizen participation. Politics as the driver of democracy should strive for common good aims, rights and humanity in the area/country served and across the rest of the world that we share.

The UK can and should evolve, develop and implement at all levels of democratic and political structures new approaches and service standards to enhance democracy and engage citizens more in the policy making and review processes.

Based on the above blueprint a letter, proposed MP code of conduct and a democratic survey was posted to all 650 MPs in 2011:

Submission to all 650 MPs 1st August 2011:

1. Consensus Objectives:

Would you support the objective of a new and enhanced democratic and political model designed by/endorsed by the people, totally accountable to the people, which seeks to deliver positive outcomes for all mankind and planet Earth ?.

2. Consensus Vision:

Would you support the vision of: Political and democratic renewal in the UK as a world-class benchmark and model for existing and emerging democracies world-wide ?.

3. Consensus Principles:

Would you consider/review each component in the principles below ?. (As first draft to be progressed by citizens with politicians, which specifies key benchmark principles of purpose and the commitment to democratic excellence:)

3.1 Politics is the management of finite resources to meet the infinite needs of people and planet.
3.2 Politics is the power entrusted to the few to work solely for the common good of the many.
3.3 Politics should provide the foundation to make a positive difference to the lives of others.
3.4 Politics is the system that seeks to deliver the democratic will of the people.
3.5 Political structures must be a benchmark for world-class democratic excellence and standards.

3.6 Overall political direction and policy-making should be conducted within a framework that puts citizens first before party or power aspirations.

4. Consensus Framework:

Do you agree that consensus politics should be based on the following five linked key components:
4.1 Commitment: to putting people first above political party/personal advancement to manage resources and work for the common good of people represented, all mankind and planet Earth.
4.2 Policy development: formulated wherever possible in consultation with/reflecting the democratic will of the people.
4.3 Planning: to ensure in a cost effective and timely way that those agreed policies are translated into plans that are costed, practical and achievable.
4.4 Action: to implement those policies within an agreed timeframe and cost.
4.5 Evaluation*: of elected representatives/their policies and performance by the people at periodic intervals.*(eg: annually as an appraisal, using such methods as public forums, online consultations/surveys etc and annual reviews by existing and developing digital technology, web-voting etc).

5. Consensus Strategy:
Which of the following strategy developments would you support:

5.1 Consultation: With the electorate/political stakeholders in democracy on Consensus aims. (Leading to eventual development of the Consensus vision, framework and principles by the electorate, political parties/movements and independents).

5.2 Consensus Think Tank: A citizen led think-tank established. An overarching centre/resource for political and democratic development.

5.3 IPADE: A development resource to build skills and high standards for current and future representatives of the people: (The Institute of Political and Democratic Excellence).

5.4 Investor In Democracy Standard: An agreed vision, a framework and citizen focussed standard for individuals seeking public office/serving as representatives of the people.

5.5 MP Code Of Conduct/Covenant with the people: A professional service standard - citizen originated for MPs/Representatives etc to endorse/be evaluated on. This defines the electorate expectations of the standards and service required.

5.6 Shadow Parliamentary Commissioner for Standards: Independent from the political establishment/elected and supported by stakeholders in democracy.

5.7 An agreed/published MP Description/service level expectations. Backed with annual reviews/appraisals by constituent input: eg web voting/digital democracy.

5.8 The People's Vote: To support above - a web-site facility for the electorate to present initiatives, appraise MPs/Representative etc and vote by email/text on local/regional/national/international issues and policies.

5.9 Constituency (Area or region linkage) Development Plan: With clear objectives/milestones drafted by MP/MP support team in consultation with local stakeholders. (within first year of the new Parliament).

5.10 Fixed Terms Of Parliament - Four Years: To provide more regular review of MP and Government performance by the electorate.

5.11 Facility for recall of MP and by-election: Triggered by agreed consensus in the constituency that the MP is not providing the service levels, commitment and standards expected by the local electorate.

5.12 Shadow MP facility in constituency: As needs arise. Eg: If MP is unable to deliver a constituency focus and presence.

5.13 Vested Interest Safeguards: To enforce/strengthen restrictions on public servants - (MPs/Ministers/civil servants) taking up paid positions as consultants/directors/employees etc in any company/organisation, which they in their public service role had, or would have influence in awarding contracts etc. (Eg resulting in previous or future commercial/financial benefit for those companies and ex-public servants/politicians).

5.14 Value For Money Safeguards: To promote safeguards/freedom of information to ensure elected representatives - MPs, Ministers (and civil servants) etc do not incur excessive costs on purchases, services and expenses. eg: unnecessary travel abroad that cannot be justified by cost-benefit review.

5.15 Consensus Community Resource Database*: To encourage supporters of democratic renewal (Inc. Political party members etc) to register voluntary offers of support/expertise to the community. *(Please Note: This Initiative previously rejected by two main British political parties)

As of October 2011 only two Labour Party MPs endorsed the code, with only six MPs responding to the survey supplied to all MPs. Perhaps the other 648 MPs were all on a long summer holiday.....There are solutions to widespread electorate despair at failures in our political and democratic systems. The people must lead now as the political species have consistently failed to deliver a world class system for the common good. The many democratic think tanks and democratic lobby groups with concerned stakeholder citizens around the country must work together on shared aims. They must agree a new way forward with a democratic blueprint based on common good values, high standards and true and timely accountability. The challenge is that the people must drive this process and right the wrongs in our current systems. Our alleged democracy should not be taken for granted as in tablets of stone.

Fellow mankind in places like Syria, Libya and Egypt have given their lives for freedom and democracy and we owe much to them and their families. We should offer emerging democracies ongoing support and resource building and indeed seek to implement a higher standard of democracy here in the UK. A democratic model, which is truly world class and a template for other nations to consider. A democratic and political system for all citizens to be proud of.

Lightning Source UK Ltd.
Milton Keynes UK
UKHW011951151122
412254UK00002B/140